S0-AJX-356

Stephanie Pui-Mun Law

STEPHANIE PUI-MUN LAW has been painting fantastic otherworlds from early childhood, though her art career did not begin until 1998, when she graduated from a program of computer science. After three years of programming for a software company by day and rushing home to paint into the midnight hours, she left the world of typed logic and numbers for the painted worlds of dreams and the fey.

Her illustrations have been for various game and publishing clients, including Wizards of the Coast, HarperCollins, LUNA Books, Tachyon Books, Alderac Entertainment, and Green Ronin. She has authored and illustrated *Dreamscapes* (2008, North Light Books), a book on watercolor technique for fantasy. Her work also regularly appears in the magazines *Realms of Fantasy*, *Cricket*, and *Cicada*.

In addition to the commissioned projects, she has spent a great deal of time working up a personal body of work whose inspiration stems from mythology, legend, and folklore. She has also been greatly influenced by the art of the Impressionists, Pre-Raphaelites, Surrealists, and the master hand of nature. Swirling echoes of sinuous oak branches, watermarked leaf stains, and the endless palette of the skies are her signature. Her background of over a decade as a flamenco dancer is also evident in the movement and composition of her paintings. Every aspect of her paintings moves in a choreographed flow—and the dancers are not only those with human limbs.

ABOUT AUTHOR
Barbara Moore

𝒯AROT, ORACLES, AND MAGIC have all influenced Barbara's life for nearly twenty years. She has studied under some of the most influential tarot experts in the world and continues to teach and work with some of the brightest stars in the field.

Barbara enjoys the challenge of giving a voice to tarot cards and oracle decks. She has had the good fortune to write books for several decks, including *A Guide to the Mystic Faerie Tarot* (Mystic Faerie Tarot), *The Gilded Tarot Companion* (Gilded Tarot), *The Witchy Tarot* (Tarot for Hip Witches), *Destiny's Portal* (The Enchanted Oracle), *The Dreamer's Journal* (Mystic Dreamer Tarot), and *Vampires Tarot of the Eternal Night*, as well as a book of magic for the *Pagan Magical Kit*. Currently, she is designing several different tarot decks and working on *Tarot for Beginners* (Llewellyn, November 2010).

Shadowscapes Tarot

STEPHANIE PUI-MUN LAW

Text by
Stephanie
Pui-Mun Law
& Barbara Moore

Llewellyn Publications
WOODBURY, MINNESOTA

FIRST EDITION
Second Printing, 2010

Artwork © 2010 Stephanie Pui-Mun Law
Book design by Rebecca Zins
Cover design by Lisa Novak

Llewellyn is a registered trademark of Llewellyn Worldwide Ltd.

. . . .

ISBN 978-0-7387-1579-7
The *Shadowscapes Tarot* kit consists of a boxed set of
78 full-color cards and this perfect-bound book.

. . . .

Llewellyn Worldwide does not participate in, endorse, or have any authority or responsibility concerning private business transactions between our authors and the public.

All mail addressed to the author is forwarded, but the publisher cannot, unless specifically instructed by the author, give out an address or phone number.

Any Internet references contained in this work are current at publication time, but the publisher cannot guarantee that a specific location will continue to be maintained. Please refer to the publisher's website for links to authors' websites and other sources.

Llewellyn Publications
A Division of Llewellyn Worldwide Ltd.
2143 Wooddale Drive
Woodbury, MN 55125-2989
www.llewellyn.com
Printed in the United States of America

Contents

Artist's Note

As I PAINT the finishing touches on the last of the kings and lay down my brush, my mind wanders back to June 2004, when I began this journey. Like the Fool, I stood on the precipice of this project, teetering on the edge of a vast unknown —this self-made challenge to my mind and my skills as an artist. And now, seventy-eight paintings later, I feel each card has been imbued with an indelible piece of my life as I made that trek. Each one bears the mark of my meditations as I wandered through a changing landscape of existence. The haunting call of loons at dusk echoes across the mirror-smooth surface of Lake Manitou and into the frame of the Hermit card. The spider who patiently spun her intricate web across my doorstep to show me what a true craftsman the Eight of Pentacles should be. The Queen of Cups, who danced into being when my inspiration was at its lowest ebb.

I've always loved stories. The archetypes of myth, legend, and fairy tales wend their way through my thoughts and into the images I create. Stories are at the heart of each of these cards—some of them my own, some of them etched in time by the voices of one storyteller to the next at bedsides and fireplaces. These tales have always been the expressions of human experiences, desires, and fears. They know no boundaries.

It is with a mixture of relief and trepidation that I sign the last card; relief that I have been able to see the journey through to its completion, and trepidation at the thought of "Where do I go from here?" The blank canvases stare at me. I look around, and the emptiness of unlimited possibilities is daunting.

But then the Fool smiles at me, takes me by the hand, and leads me to the edge of the shifting mists. "Take a new leap," she says.

Introduction

BY BARBARA MOORE

*B*EFORE YOU DO anything else, here is what you must do. This magical deck deserves a magical moment, a moment between you and it. You must form a first impression of each other. Each card in this deck is like a door and can open up worlds. Like two strangers catching each other's eyes across a room in a glance of just the briefest of moments that holds so many possibilities, that will be you and this deck in about two minutes.

Take your deck and shuffle it—or not, whichever you prefer—close your eyes, and pick one card. Finish this paragraph and then put the book down. Ignore the name and number on the card and just look at the picture. Drink it in. Revel in the intricate yet simple beauty of it. Look at it for so long that you can see it with your eyes closed. Then close your eyes, still seeing the card. Step into the image. Imagine how it feels, how it smells, how it sounds. Experience it. If you're feeling adventurous, interact with a figure in the image. After you are done, come back to the book.

Many people, especially those new to tarot, wonder where the meanings for cards come from. The meanings are made up of a collage of different things, and now you know one of them. You just experienced a card. What did that experience mean? Whatever it meant to you, that is part of the meaning of the card.

Ironically, for many people this is both the hardest and the easiest part of the meaning. To simply look at a picture and say what it means is something children do all the time, but adults seem to struggle with it, as if afraid to "get it wrong." Intuition and emotional response are important to tarot reading and work hand in hand with the intellectual interpretations. As you will see, tarot is very much about balance ... the balance of your heart and mind, your spirit and your body.

Tarot is a combination of structure and art that creates a unique experience. When all of you—your heart, mind, body, and spirit—is engaged, you are in a numinous place. You become open to the wisdom that is hidden within yourself. This is how the tarot helps answer questions and provides guidance. The answers and guidance don't come from the cards; the cards are a tool. The answers are in you; the cards help you see the answers.

In the pages ahead, you will learn some tarot basics that will provide a foundation from which your intuition can fly. There are also complete instructions for doing a tarot reading. Then you will find in-depth card interpretations beautifully written by the artist herself. These interpretations will give more depth to the card meanings and make your experience even more powerful. At the end of the book, there is a collection of spreads to use. You'll be ready to do your own readings and find the answers you are looking for.

You are about to start a journey of self-discovery with a collection of images created to inspire and a book that provides signposts. They will get you on your way, but where you go is entirely up to you!

Tarot Basics

Reading tarot is a very personal experience. Every reader has their own style, influenced by their beliefs, their knowledge, and their skill. But even people reading for the first time have meaningful and useful interactions with the cards. Without reading another word, you could ask a question, pull one card, look at the picture, and find an answer. But the more you know, the easier and deeper your readings will be.

This chapter will show you how to develop your interpretation skills by showing how different things shape card meanings. You will also find guidance on how to perform a reading. But remember, tarot reading is personal. As you practice and gain experience, you will find what works for you and what doesn't.

Making Meanings

Doing a tarot reading is based on interpreting the cards that are dealt to answer a particular question. An interpretation for a card is slightly different every time it turns up. This is because many factors affect what the card means; for example:

- Your reaction to the art.
- Your intuition.
- The card name or suit designation.
- Traditional meanings.
- The artist's intention and unique vision of the card.
- The question asked.
- The position of the card in the spread.

As you can see, the meaning of any card is a complex layering of history, structure, artistic interpretation, context, and emotional response.

Deck Structure

Let's start with the structure of a tarot deck. You may have noticed that there are lots of tarot decks available, as well as other types of "oracle" decks. A tarot deck, as opposed to an oracle deck, has a very specific structure. Understanding this structure will add to your ability to interpret the cards.

The structure is easy—assuming you are familiar with a regular deck of playing cards. A tarot deck has something in common with a playing card deck. It can be seen as two parts, each called an *arcana*. Arcana means "secret." One part, the Major Arcana, we'll discuss in a moment. The other part, the Minor Arcana, has four suits named wands, cups, swords, and pentacles, whereas a playing card deck has clubs, hearts, spades, and diamonds. Each suit has cards numbered from ace to ten. Here's where it gets a little different: a playing card deck has a jack, queen, and king. A tarot deck has a page, knight, queen, and king—four royals (or court cards, as they're called in tarot) instead of three.

Each of the suits is associated with an element (fire, water, air, or earth) and represents an area of human experience. Wands are associated with fire and represent passion, activities, and projects. Cups are associated with water and represent relationships, emotions, and creativity. Swords are associated with air and represent challenges/problems, thoughts, and the intellect. Pentacles are associated with earth and represent resources, physical things, and the body. The Minor Arcana, as you can tell by the name, represents small secrets, or aspects of our everyday lives.

The Minor Arcana cards have numbers or court card names on them. These also have meanings:

ACES: new beginnings, potential

TWOS: duality, balance, relationship

THREES: creativity, birth, growth

FOURS: stability, structure, stagnation

FIVES: conflict, uncertainty, instability

SIXES: communication, problem solving, equilibrium

SEVENS: reflection, assessment, evaluation

EIGHTS: movement, power, progress

NINES: compromises, compassion, spirituality

TENS: completion, perfection, end of a cycle

PAGES: youthful enthusiasm, a message

KNIGHTS: extreme, fast, quest, rescue

QUEENS: mature, caring, experienced

KINGS: leader, protector, authority

As you interpret the cards, consider the suit and the number or name as well as your intuitive and emotional response to the art. Use each of these components in the final interpretation—but not *only* these; the question and the position in the spread will play a role as well. Before we look at those, let's talk about the Major Arcana.

The High Priestess, the Wheel of Fortune, Death, the Lovers … these cards are part of the mysterious Major Arcana. Well, they are considered mysterious by some, and it's true—their names do have a very esoteric and exciting feel. The Major Arcana cards are the "big secrets." Unlike the Minor Arcana that focus on everyday events, the Major Arcana represent milestones, major or dramatic events, spiritual aspects, and things beyond our control.

The Major Arcana cards are numbered from zero (the Fool) to twenty-one (the World). They all have a name and traditionally are numbered with a roman numeral. While these cards are complex, you can get a feel for their basic meaning from their name. The Fool is someone naive, innocent, and perhaps, well, foolish. The High Priestess is someone with deep, intuitive knowledge. The Wheel of Fortune is about changes in fortune and the cycles of life. The Moon is about dreams, shadows, and deception.

When Major Arcana cards show up in your readings, keep in mind that they represent significant events or experiences. Consider the card's name as you examine the image and include it in your interpretation.

Traditional Meanings and the Artist's Vision

In addition to the structural meanings, tarot cards have, over time, developed what many consider their "traditional" meanings. In the card section of this book, Stephanie has included the traditional meanings. In addition to these traditional meanings, she has written supplemental text that gives voice to the cards, to help guide you into a deeper experience and understanding of her vision of the cards and, we hope, into your own personal relationship with the cards. The cards, particularly the Major Arcana, can have layers of meanings and ways to view those meanings, so each tarot artist shows a particular facet. For example, the Hierophant has to do with traditional teachings. Depending on the point of view, this can be stagnating and repressive or comforting and enriching. Each tarot artist will have a perspective that is uniquely their own. And it is made even more unique by your response to the image, the name, and the traditional meaning.

The Question

Asking the right question is important because it will shape the answer. The whole "what's the right question" thing is tricky. Everyone has their own ideas about the best ways to ask questions. Here are some things to think about as you frame your question.

1. Don't ask if you don't want to know

Seriously. Imagine all the possible answers to your question that you can, good and bad and neutral. How would you feel if any one of those were the answer? If you are ready to know, no matter what, then ask. If not, put it off until you are ready.

2. Do you believe the future is predetermined?

If you want to ask the cards something about what is going to happen in the future, then it can be assumed that you believe your future is set or fated, that you do not have free will and cannot affect outcomes—in short, you believe whatever is going to happen is going to happen. This belief will have an effect on the way you phrase your question. You are more likely to ask, "Will I ever get married?" as opposed to "How can I attract a strong relationship into my life?"

3. Do you believe that you have total control over your future?

This is just the opposite of the above belief. In this case, your questions about the future might focus on what actions you can take to create what you want. You may ask, "How can I find the job of my dreams?" as opposed to "Will I ever find a job?"

4. Do you believe that you have some control but some things are beyond your control?

This is a hybrid approach, and it is a popular one. If you believe that you do have much control over your life but also believe that there are some things that you cannot control, then you might ask different questions. You may ask multi-tiered questions, such as "What do I need to know about the job market, and how can I find the best job for me?"

The question is important. It not only reflects your beliefs and shapes the answer, it also affects the way you interpret the cards. For example, someone who favors a predetermined belief system might interpret the Death card in a romance reading as the end of the relationship. Someone working from a more control-focused belief may read the card as an opportunity to transform a stagnant situation. In one reading, the person *experiences* something; in the other, the person *does* something.

Position in the Spread

A spread is the way the cards are laid out in a reading. There are lots of different spreads designed for lots of different readings. There is a collection of spreads in this book that you can use. There are books of spreads you can buy. There are free spreads that you can find online. You can even invent your own spreads.

Each position in a spread is assigned a meaning. For example, a simple three-card spread is this:

1. Past
2. Present
3. Future

The first card represents what happened in the past; the second, what is happening now; and the third, what will happen (or is likely to happen) in the future. In this spread, it is easy to see how the positions would subtly affect card interpretation.

Another variation of the three-card spread looks like this:

1. The problem
2. Advice
3. Likely outcome

In this spread, the effect is less subtle. Reading a card for advice (position 2) is different from reading it as a potential outcome (position 3). The Moon card as advice might be read as "trust your dreams" or "don't reveal everything." As an outcome card, though, it might be read as "beware of illusions or deceptions."

A Word about Reversals

As you continue your exploration of tarot, you will likely hear about "reversed" cards. Reversed cards are cards that are upside down in a spread. That is, they are face up, but the bottom of the card is oriented at the top, like this:

Upright card   Reversed card

There are differing opinions among tarot readers about reversed cards. Some readers do not interpret reversed cards differently but instead just turn them upright and continue on. Others keep the cards reversed and interpret them differently than if they were upright. Some deck designers intend the cards to be read reversed and so include those meanings in the book. Stephanie did not design this deck to use reversed cards, so those meanings are not included.

If you desire to incorporate reversed cards into your interpretation process, you can try various techniques. For more information, check out Mary K. Greer's *Complete Book of Tarot Reversals*. In it, she teaches various methods for interpreting reversed cards. Some ideas include interpreting the card as if upright but paying special attention to it, interpreting the card as blocked or repressed, or interpreting the card as the opposite of the upright meaning.

Now that you have lots of information to use for making meanings for the individual cards, you might want to just spend time looking at your cards, getting first impressions, and maybe jotting down some notes about your initial ideas. Or you might want to move on and jump right into doing a reading.

Readings

Readings are the process of using tarot cards to determine answers to questions. Readings can be as simple or elaborate as you like. In this section, we'll outline the very basic elements of a simple reading. Then we'll share some ideas that you might want to incorporate into your readings ... or that might inspire you to come up with some of your own.

Basic Reading Steps

1. Determine the question

Many people choose to write it down, along with the cards drawn, their positions, and their interpretations, for later reference.

2. Pick a spread

Select a spread that will best answer your question, or create your own spread.

3. Shuffle the cards

There are many ways to shuffle, so use whatever method you are comfortable with, or experiment, if you like.

4. Lay the cards in the spread positions

To start with, lay the cards face up, and deal them off the top of the deck. We'll discuss options for this step below.

5. Interpret the cards individually

Go through the cards one by one and determine their meanings.

6. Synthesize the reading into an answer

Combine all the cards, keeping in mind their positions, into a meaningful answer to the question.

———

And that's it. That is the least you need to do in order to perform a reading. However, there is much room for variation, and there are many options to make the experience more powerful and more meaningful.

Beyond the Basics

Rituals

Rituals are not a necessary part of doing a reading. There are, though, a few good reasons for incorporating a ritual or two into your reading practice. Our days and lives are busy, and distractions abound. Even the simplest ritual is a way to calm down, center yourself, and focus on the task at hand. Some think of a tarot reading as a connection or communication with the divine. This communication benefits from an open state of mind, where your everyday logic is a little quieted and your intuitive mind is more activated. Performing a ritual before a reading lets your mind know to rearrange itself and get into reading mode. Finally, if you are reading for someone, performing a ritual helps them calm, center, and focus too. It allows them to enter a numinous state, so that they are more open to receiving the message from their reading.

Rituals can be as elaborate or simple as you wish. Your pre-reading ritual can be just one act or a series of actions. Here is a list of things that other readers do. Try a few, individually or in combinations, and see what feels right for you.

- Spread out a special cloth to lay the cards on.
- Shuffle and cut your cards the same way every time.
- Place your feet flat on the floor, clasp your hands in your lap, close your eyes, and center yourself.
- Light a candle.
- Play some music.
- Say a prayer or affirmation.
- Burn incense.

Shuffling, Cutting, and Dealing

Before doing a reading, randomize your deck by shuffling the cards. There are many ways to shuffle. You can riffle the cards, as many people do when playing card games. If you are concerned that this method will warp your cards, you can use the overhand shuffle. If you find the cards too long (or your hands too small) for the overhand, you can use the mud pie method of spreading all the cards face down on the table and moving them around with the palms of your hands.

Cutting the cards is fairly straightforward. In game play, cutting the cards plays a role in preventing cheating, but if incorporated into a tarot reading, it is mostly just part of the ritual. Divide the deck into two or more piles, and then pick them back up in any order. Some readers do this with their non-dominant hand.

Dealing the cards is how you take the individual cards from the pile and move them to their position in the spread. You can deal from the top of the deck or the bottom of the deck. You can fan out the cards on the table, select the number needed for the spread at random, gather them into a pile, and deal from the top or bottom.

If you are reading for someone else, decide whether only you will shuffle and cut the cards, if just the person asking the question will, or if you both will. Some people don't let anyone else touch their cards. Others think it is important to get both parties' energies mixed into the cards.

Some people favor dealing the cards face up, some face down. Dealing the cards face down has the advantages of building a sense of mystery and drama as each card is revealed and of keeping the focus on one card at a time and not being distracted by cards that come later. Dealing face up has the advantage of allowing you to scan the reading as a whole and gain general information about the reading before delving into the specific cards.

Scanning the Reading

Scanning the reading is a simple technique that lets you form an overview of the information provided in the spread. Because you know that different groups of cards in the deck have specific meanings, you can incorporate your knowledge of the basic structure of a tarot deck. Major Arcana cards represent major life events, cups represent emotions and relationships, aces represent new beginnings, etc.

There are other things some tarot readers watch for. If there are a lot of court cards, it could mean too many people are involved in the situation. Knights can mean a situation is fast-moving (especially with an Eight of Wands). Aces, twos, and threes can mean a situation is in its early stages; fours, fives, and sixes, in the middle; sevens, eights, and nines, nearing resolution; tens show the end of a situation or cycle. When you lay out a spread, look for multiple Major Arcana cards, suits, numbers, or court cards. You can also scan for colors, symbols, or images that repeat and speak to your intuition.

If, for example, you are doing a reading about a relationship and there are many swords, no cups, and a few fours, there is the overall sense that things are not well—there are problems and probably stagnation. Then, as you interpret each card in its position, you add in the details.

Cleansing

Cleansing your deck is similar to doing a ritual, only it's something you do after the reading, not before. This is a way to symbolically and energetically rid your cards of unwanted influences and reset the deck to a neutral state. You can go through your deck and put all the cards upright and in order. Pass the cards through the smoke of burning sage or incense. Store your cards with a clear or rose quartz. Put your deck on a windowsill (inside!) in the light of the full moon.

Keeping a Journal

Many tarot readers record their readings in a journal. For them, it is a learning tool. By keeping track of your readings, you can go back later and see how the situations that you read about turned out. You can see if your interpretations were accurate or if you missed a particular meaning in the reading.

Another favorite journal technique is to select a card a day (or however often you like) and use the card as inspiration for a free-writing session. Free writing is picking a time limit—try starting with five minutes—and writing without regard to grammar, spelling, or anything. Just keep writing whatever thoughts the card inspires. After your free writing, write out what you know about the card meaning and incorporate any insight or wisdom you gained from your free writing.

As you keep your journal, you'll be noting all your insights, revelations, and "a-ha!" moments. From time to time, go back and reread your journal. You may be surprised what you learned and then forgot or notice some grain of wisdom that you didn't realize was so wise at the time.

And now, it's time to take a peek into the notebook of the artist, to get her ideas, full of wisdom and beautifully written, about the cards she's so magically and carefully created.

The Major Arcana

0 The Fool

$\mathcal{I}$T BEGINS WITH a whispered voice. The serpentine song threads through her days and her thoughts. It beckons: *Come ... come ... come ...* "Where?" she asks, curious, but there is no response.

She ignores the summons, until one day that siren song unexpectedly explodes and fills her to the brim. Its pulse is undeniable. "Where?" she asks again, and this time the steady beat of her heart is the response.

The Fool has come a long way, traveled from far beyond to come to this pinnacle that rises up upon the edge of the world, and yet her journey is just about to begin. She senses this with instinctive perceptions as she rises up on her toes, caught up in the breathless embrace of the wind in the moment before the plunge. Her heart pounds and flutters in her chest with the force of a hundred beating wings struggling to break free of the cage of her being, until she feels she must be sprouting wings from her shoulders to glide forth from that place, transformed.

Wait! Don't! cries a thin, trailing voice from within. *Caution! Fear!* it rails. *Hold back!*

Unheeding, she steps forward, and ...

Meaning: She stands on the edge of a very sheer precipice, with only the ribbons and the doves bearing her up if she chooses to leap. The fox takes this in. He watches. He is the embodiment of cleverness, but being clever does not preclude being a fool of a different sort. He can't comprehend the leap of faith that she is about to take. So who's the fool, she for stepping out into the unknown, in what seems to be a complete lack of logic, or the fox for being too firmly rooted in the belief of the reality of intellectual thought?

The Fool is a symbol for new beginnings and adventures, pleasure, passion. She rushes ahead, thoughtless and rash, doing before thinking, obeying instincts. Like the Fool, you may stand upon the precipice gazing out into the unknown. The endless expanse of blue nothing is all that fills the space between that high-up aerie and the ground that is so very far away. There is either an oblivious foolishness to the terrible plunge you may experience, or else a wild spirit of adventure and great faith and knowledge in what can and will bear you up and guide you through the times to come. There are unlimited possibilities opening up for the seeker.

I The Magician

THE FOOL DRIFTS past as a seed in the wind, as a twirling feather, as a crystal mote of condensation, and she sees the Magician. She watches the boy who is initiated into the mysteries of the elements. He is taught and masters conjurings, summonings, bindings.

One day she cannot resist, and she trails fingers of wind across his eyes; he opens them with a start, seeing for a moment. "Who are you?" he demands, but oh so quickly the spirit transforms into a stag and bounds away.

He chases the stag into the woods. Always the stag is just out of reach. His bare feet press into the earth. The air rushes through his hair. The sun beats upon his shoulders. The tantalizing flash of white from the stag darting through the verdure taunts him unbearably until suddenly...

It is gone, and he is alone.

Upon a rock, he sees the gifts that have been left for him. The relics of the elements glint in the sunlight, and as his hands close upon the offerings, a smile touches his lips at the power that surges through them.

Meaning: Originality, creativity, skill, willpower, self-confidence, dexterity, and sleight of hand. It is about grasping the unseen around you and harnessing it to become reality, drawing forth the ineffable into the material realm of existence. This Magician draws upon relics representative of the elements: fire in his lantern, the voice of the sea in the shell, a breath of wind in the raven's feather, and earth from the leaves. He knows what he wants, and he knows he can make it happen with conscious exertion of his will and his knowledge of how to manipulate the world.

II The High Priestess

$\mathcal{T}$HE HIGH PRIESTESS opens herself to the sky. She basks in the radiance the stars cast upon her upturned cheeks. She soaks in that tremulous, incandescent light, feeling it glow within her mind, opening corridors and dancing into filigree patterns.

The stars chant:

> We were here when the mountains were young
> and the sea was only a dream...
> we've seen the hills bloom with countless millions of seasons...
> we've watched the clouds paint their visions
> in a slow language across the centuries...
> let us speak.

The owl hoots in the darkness, calling out to his mistress with the music of the night. His white feathers gleam in the moonlight, as if with a light from within. He glides through the darkness to come to rest near her.

In the gloam, the night is full of whispers—the secret knowledge of the stars, of the trees, and of the earth. The spirits of each murmur their collected stories and their wisdom in a sibilant descant.

She weaves those sounds through her fingers, drawing the voices into physical being, and in her fingers, a filigree key coalesces. She calls the owl to her. "Take this, and be the bearer of secrets," she tells him.

Meaning: Wisdom, knowledge, learning, intuition, purity, virtue. The High Priestess lifts her arms out, and in that gesture, her very body becomes the living symbol of a chalice. The owl is a keeper of knowledge, and he bears a key to unlock mysteries. The pomegranate is an icon of Persephone, who tasted the seeds and thus tied herself to Hades; it is a fruit of fertility and death. The moons embroidered upon her garments wax and wane, the new crescent and gibbous moons that create the full cycle embraced in one.

III The Empress

ᴸADY-MOTHER!" CALL THE wandering souls. "We bring you gifts!" They fly near the Empress, dancing in the sky. They paint synchronized kaleidoscope choreographies for her pleasure, and she smiles as she takes it in. Her mind and her thoughts are the conductor to this visual symphony.

Gently, they lay a crown woven of the first buds of spring across her brow. "Jasmine and Lily of the Valley have graciously donated their first buds for your coronet," the spirits sigh.

"The Apple Tree Man has gifted you with his fruit, and the Lady of the Fields, her grains." These they lay in her basket.

With a sudden flourish, the spirits whirl together, then spin off in an explosion of light and music. "Farewell, dear Lady!" they call.

Meaning: Creativity, generosity, patience, love. The Empress is about abundance, experiencing the senses, and embracing the natural. She is a creator. She is the Mother, fertile and nurturing. Clasped to her body like a child, she holds a basket of the earth's bounty: fruits and sheaves of wheat and glorious flowers. She is the primal essence and embodiment of life, and is deeply tied to nature. Crowned in ivy, she is clasped in garments the colors of the world around her.

IV The Emperor

$\mathcal{T}$HE EMPEROR REMEMBERS ...

He remembers when once there was another man. Was it his father? A mentor? Or was it a vanquished king? His mind arcs back, grasping. Once ... there was another, and he relinquished the dragon orb.

He remembers his own fascination with the orb upon first laying eyes on it—how as he touched it, the strength of the creature within surged through his arms and possessed his senses. *You are now the lord of these mortal realms.* Was it the other who had said that? Or was it the dragon? He was now the dragon!

"Yessss," he said, and knew it was so.

Meaning: Creating order out of chaos, authority, leadership, strength, establishing law and order. The carvings on the wall bear the symbols of the domain and of dominion. The eagle ascends above mountains and sea, night and day, ruling over all. The earthly creatures bow to that mastery. But even though the imagery of the carvings may be magnificent, still a wall is a man-made edifice—man's measure and means of controlling the wildness of the world by attempting to carve it into unchanging stone, man's desire to control and etch out and write the story of his own destiny. The Emperor is a man rooted in his ways and views and regimens but confident that this is the right structure and way of things.

V The Hierophant

"𝓘 WOULD LIKE A story," says the salamander to the Hierophant.

"And what would you like to hear, little one?" The words come slowly. Each syllable seems to be drawn from deep within, pulled up from an individual rootlet. The salamander is used to it, and patient.

"I want to hear how I may fly. I was content. And then one day, my friend Caterpillar said he was sleepy. He slept for a long time, until I nearly forgot him—until yesterday. A moth came to laugh at me. He laughed with Caterpillar's laugh, and with Caterpillar's voice he said he had had a dream of wings."

"Ah." The sonorous exhalation seems to go on forever. "Ah, little one; I am sorry. Caterpillar has that blessing. He may sleep and dream of flight. He weaves a silken ritual around his body, and then comes the day when that vision transforms him. You ... "

"I wish to dream of flight too!" says Salamander, very seriously.

"You may dream of it," says his friend and teacher. "I will not be the one to deny you divinity. But just know that your own divinity shall be attained along a different path than Caterpillar's. Do not relinquish your dream, Salamander."

Meaning: The Hierophant's roots reach deep, entwined around secrets and traditions and the ages. He believes in ritual and ceremony, in pursuing knowledge and deeper meaning, and in the rigidity of a belief system. He elucidates the spiritual and brings it to the earthly plane. He is calm and in possession of himself, and he is the teacher who can help unravel mysteries.

VI The Lovers

*I*N ONE OF the oldest tales, there is the Choice: knowledge and fulfillment of worldly senses, or the simplicity of an ever-present now.

To be drawn into an embrace, to seek that union that all souls ache for and desire, to know the oneness of passion and love and revel in it. Their eyes are open, but they gaze only at each other, oblivious to the sun that goes on turning above them and the gaze of the heavens. Neither gold and gem-encrusted crown of kings nor grapevine- and flower-twined crown of peasants grace their brows, for the forces gathering around them make no such distinctions; indeed, their own senses have no awareness of such either.

"Take this seed," he says to her, placing an acorn in her palm. "Water it with the fount of your spirit and your intentions."

"And we shall see what grows of that," she replies.

Meaning: Union, balance, energy, flow, love, desire, passion, melding of heart and mind, forming a union or marriage. Though it can be romantic in nature, it is not necessarily so. The Lovers is also about determining values and struggling with choices—the innocence embodied in the turtledoves is a contrast to the shiny red apple in the embrace of the snake, one of the oldest symbols of temptation. Likewise, the pure simplicity of the calla lily contrasts the lush and sensual complexity of a rose.

VII The Chariot

SHE IS WINGED Victory, the goddess Nike, or Maeve. She comes sweeping from the skies, confident and sure of herself. She has summoned the unicorns of the sea out from the foamy depths. They serve her willingly, bowing as is ever in their nature to such purity of intent. The ocean swells themselves are tamed beneath the enchanted wheels of her chariot. The glittering waves crash and roar with the strength of the sea, but as she guides her unicorns across the glistening track, the waves fall still before her and into a quiescent and shining mirror path.

This stillness in what is in eternal motion stirs awareness in the denizens of the deep. From underneath, the spirits of the ocean whisper to the sea god, and in a swirl of aquatic color, they dance to the surface to greet one whose willpower and mastery is so undeniable as to be capable of overcoming even the wild, natural fury of the seas.

Meaning: Triumph over obstacles, achieving victory, focusing intent and will, establishing an identity, self-confidence, maintaining discipline, assuming the reins of power and authority, and driving with the unwavering certainty in a cause. Control must be exercised in a constantly changing environment that can and will present challenges—in the landscape of a world that is constantly shifting with people and emotions and circumstances all around. Like the tenuous border where sea meets sky, a constant tension of push and pull of air against liquid is maintained, and to ride to victory, one must be able to achieve the confidence and knowledge to walk upon that fragile surface.

VIII Strength

THE LION ROARS. The earth trembles, and the clouds skitter nervously. The bamboo sways gently. The Chinese know the hidden strength of bamboo: so fragile and delicate-seeming, but flexible and strong. It is a strength that does not need to shout of its power to the world but sways and bows to the wind, then springs gracefully forward again with a melodious rustle of leaves.

He roars again, and a flock of birds jolt from their perches to take flight at the sound. The maiden steps forward. She is as willowy as the stalks of the bamboo grove she emerges from. Step by step, unafraid, she approaches the beast. This king of the wilds watches her, and she meets him eye to eye.

A third time his mighty challenge echoes to the skies, in a claim of mastery and ownership and dominion to any who hear it. She smiles as she comes within arm's length, and at her touch, the great golden head bows.

Meaning: Courage, calm composure and patience, compassion, persuasion and soft control, tempered force. Managing impulses to control anger and force, rather than be manipulated by them. One must have faith in success, though it might not come at once, and it may not come very easy—the lion is fierce, and the fire he guards is a flame that burns. Strength must be tempered sometimes. Unshakable resolve is what will see through to the desired end.

There are many kinds of strength. There is fierce and bestial power, brute force of tooth and claw, the fierce winged protectiveness called forth by a swan for her young. There is the steady strength of an oak springing from a tiny acorn but growing, growing, growing into a mighty tree. There is the strength of bamboo, swaying and internalizing forces from around but not breaking.

IX The Hermit

*H*E IS THE seeker who has turned his back to the noise and light and distractions of the world. In the city, the fragile light of the stars is drowned by the glare and the haze of life.

He takes his lantern. He was told by the wise woman that it was a bit of a captured star, and it knows its way home. The lonely beam of light pulls him clear of the valleys and high above a glittering lake whose surface is a liquid mirror. His star-lantern marks the path, and he does not know where he goes, but each step lights the next, and the next, and the next.

He climbs to a distant pinnacle that is clear of the smog of humanity, and as he retreats, the air attains a spicy fragrance. It is a purity he does not know he has missed until he breathes it for the first time, and then it is as if the body aches for and cannot live without that breath of life. Others have been here before him, but the steps are pristine and there is no indication of their passage. It is the nature of the place that to each who comes, they are the first and the only, and no other will tread there until the present visitor is forgotten.

It is a long journey, and during the course of the trek, his eyes finally become accustomed to the darkness of the wild. He leaves behind his memory of the city. The star in his lantern burns hot and bright, and her sisters in the heavens swirl in a joyous dance.

Meaning: Being introspective, seeking solitude, withdrawing from the world, and giving or receiving guidance. The Hermit is an inspirational friend and teacher, and his help can illuminate the secrets of one's own mind. That which was mysterious can be made clear with the proper light to shine on the situation. The loons glide on silent wings across the horizon, elusive shadows in the night. They are symbols of peace and tranquility, and their eerily haunting call that echoes across waterways is laden with ancient wisdom. Loons are also respected for their knowledge of the sky, sea, and forest worlds, and have often been seen in the headdresses of Indian chiefs.

X The Wheel

STORYBOOKS BEGIN, "ONCE upon a time..." and then, like a neatly wrapped package, they come to "The End."

But true tales have no beginning or end. They do not exist only when men say "Exist!" but are always there, reverberating through time in a weaving dance. We try to contain it with beginnings and ends, to put boundaries on everything simply because our own lives are bounded by birth and death. And thus we seek to lessen the power of what is immortal. True tales have a power that reaches beyond.

The Fates weave the threads of life eternally, one tied to another. Snip this thread here. Weave it into the tapestry there. Slowly, as the cloth rolls away, the images emerge.

Night follows day in the cycle of the heavens. Years bloom with the first fresh buds of spring, to the sweltering profusion of long summer days, the shower of leaves as autumn sets in, and then the long, dormant wait and sleep of winter... and on it goes, and on.

It is an inexorable and timeless tale.

The walls and beauty that artisans create will one day fall, and new structures will rise up on those remains. And so do the individual fortunes of any one person, on a cycle that may last a day or two, or years on end. Change will come.

Meaning: The Wheel of Fortune—
Destiny—the weaving of life's threads coming
together, fate, turning points, movement and
change, patterns and cycles, an interconnected
world. The knotwork in the stained glass window
circles around the wheel as a single golden thread
without start or finish. The rise and fall of the
wheel as it turns is as the changes of life. If the
world seems to be closing in and crushing hope
with its weight, step back to see the bigger picture
and the upturn that is soon to come.

XI Justice

To the Egyptians, when death claimed a soul, one was brought to be judged by the goddess Ma'at. She weighed the soul on her scales against a feather, and if found wanting, that soul was sent to the underworld.

There are those who say Justice is blind, but that is not so. Her eyes blaze white, not with blindness but with the pure white of truth. She sees through mere flesh, peeling aside the layers of emotion, dissemination, illusion, and perception, and into the heart, where the unfettered awareness resides. There is no hiding. She stands for karma. The souls gathered in the butterflies hover near, and she bears the feather close to her heart, like a sword.

She judges not with her own bias or with grays of maybes, but in terms of stark black and white. Things are as they are—fair, impartial, and right. And there is a balance that is achieved when true justice has been meted out, an evening-out of what was not settled correctly.

Meaning: Balance, harmony, equilibrium, assuming responsibility, weighing all sides of an issue before making a decision, choosing with full awareness. Justice relies on a logical mind, capable of objective ruling on situations and adjusting what needs reassessment. Meditation on right, morality, and duty, and perhaps compromise must be made in order to truly even both sides of a situation. Admit and acknowledge the truth. Comprehend the results of your actions and the connections they have to everything around, and from that, set a course for the future.

XII The Hanged Man

$\mathcal{I}_N$ THE FOGGY depths of the woods, he dips his fingers into the red clay, and with a careful hand he trails the patterns across his skin, across chest and arms and face. The spirals of red draw his mind into that place of deep meditation where thought becomes action and where the stillness speaks with the voices of the gods.

When the silence in his soul is absolute, he rises to his feet. The spirits of the forest watch as he passes, in mute witness and respect. They reach out tentatively to touch his hallowed flesh and fall into his footsteps. With solemn dignity, the procession arrives at the great oak.

The Hanged Man makes his choice of self-sacrifice. He goes willingly to his fate, unhinges his grip on control, and endures for the sake of the rewards such knowing sacrifice may bring. Ivy creeps along his body, binding and entwining him physically to the tree, until they are as one. Ivy, symbol of determination and the unbreakable strength and will of the human spirit.

In an echo of his action of faith and sacrifice, the fey fold back their wings and free-fall from their perches in the tree, entrusting themselves to the winds.

Meaning: Letting go and surrendering to experience and emotional release. Accepting what is, and giving up control. Suspending action. Sacrifice. As Odin hung upon the World Tree, Yggdrasil, in his quest for knowledge, thus to attain the greatest rewards, one must be willing to give up the self. The Hanged Man also urges you to reverse your view of the world and see things in a new light. Sometimes a change in one's perception of the world is required, a subtle shifting of the state of mind.

XIII Death

$\mathcal{I}$T IS SAID that the swan is mute its entire life. Upon the threshold of death, however, it sings one achingly beautiful song that steals the final breath from its chest, and then it expires upon that ultimate sigh. It is the most heartbreakingly wrenching song of ending.

But the song of the phoenix ... ah, the song of the swan cannot compare. When the phoenix sees death beckoning, she lifts her voice in a tragic song of pain, of rending, of sorrow ... that yet cannot mask the most intense joy, for she knows that as the flames lick at her heart, the heat is quickening the egg in which her successor sleeps. Her deathflame is its lifespark; one is linked inextricably to the other. And thus she was tied to her predecessor, and she hers, and she hers, to the beginning of time. She sits in her deathbed, upon her nest, and she submits to the inevitable hand of fate. As the fire burns searing hot and white, she spreads her wings and breathes her final song of expiration.

Meaning: Closing the door to the past and opening a new one, going through transition, changing status, shedding the old and excess, bowing to inexorable forces and sweeping changes. The old must be set aside and burned away to make way for the new. The ancient story of the phoenix is one that is echoed and repeated in dozens of cultures. She is death and rebirth and life, encapsulated in a single symbol. Irises are associated with death, as Iris was the Greek goddess of the rainbow, which she used to travel down to earth with messages from the gods and to transport women's souls to the underworld. Deadly nightshade is a highly poisonous plant, symbol of deception, danger, and death. And sumac, in the Victorian language of flowers, says, "I shall survive the change."

XIV Temperance

SHE GATHERS HERSELF, reaches within for the calm center, that place of balance. From her center, she feels the dragon and phoenix stirring. They twine about one another. They embrace in a sinuous twisting of scale and feather until it seems that one melts into the other. They coil around each other in a timeless battle for supremacy, choreographed in an elegant waltz of give and take, push and pull. They swirl about her in a maelstrom that assaults the senses. Like a maestro, she watches over and reins in one or the other when she senses any imbalance so that harmony is maintained.

Earth and sky, fire and water, male and female, summer's warmth and lush growth and winter's chill winds bearing down: these opposites flow one into the other in the cyclical and endless push of yin and yang. They are perfectly balanced against one another; in fact, they are given purpose and definition by the existence of diametric opposites.

Without water, fire rages utterly unchecked and all-consuming, burning itself out eventually in a terrible conflagration. And without fire, the waters are lightless and drowning, flooding until there is only a still, silent mirror of nothing. By defining each other's limits, they both become imbued with life and become life-giving, tempered to co-exist in just the right balance, for too much of one, and the other will be smothered.

Meaning: Harmony and equilibrium, balancing of opposites, healing. Moderation of extremes, self-restraint, harnessing absolute forces, and reining them in to be wielded to a purpose. Holding opposites apart from one another denies their power of unity. By drawing them together to merge in a measured fashion, and understanding what one bestows upon the other, a beautiful synthesis can be created. Sometimes all that holds the two apart is a wall of belief. Being flexible and understanding that there is more than one way to perceive the world can go a long way towards breaking down that invisible wall.

XV The Devil

SHE FEELS THE walls closing in on her, oblivious to the fact that she is not completely surrounded—there is the wide world open to either side! The skies cry with songs of beauty and freedom, but she tucks her head down to hide in fear, bound within walls and shackles, though it is only a thin thread that binds her, red as her heart's blood, and the key is so close, so close. *Look up!* you wish to cry at her. *Raise your eyes and look around!*

But her ears are deaf to any voice but that of the Devil. All she hears and feels is the Devil dancing above her, driving her, goading her, pressing down upon her. *Tap tap tap* goes the dancing of his hooves in a merry, mocking rhythm. *Tap tap tap* in the seductive patterns of entrapment of the willing. *Tap tap tap* he dances, and he laughs with the knowledge that it is with such ease he can hold a vibrant spirit captive.

Look up! Faintly, the voice pierces through the stones and seeps up into her body, and she reaches out.

Meaning: Losing independence, addiction and enslavement, caught up in the material realm, overindulgence, choosing to stay in the dark, pleasures, lust, and desire. Feeling hopelessness close in and limit the options. The Devil plays on your desires with a masterful touch. Break free from the puppeteer's strings by looking beyond the material blockades and temptations.

XVI The Tower

$\mathcal{A}$ SEED DRIFTS DOWN on the wind, deposited lightly to the ground. From it a tree takes root. As the years turn, it grows—a slender sapling, glowing with green life. And the years turn—grand and stately, it reaches to the sky, challenges the heavens. And the years turn—it is a mighty giant among giants, lovingly crafted living wood and greenery that is Nature's masterpiece.

Birds come to rest in its glorious limbs, joyous and singing, full of songs inspired by the heat of sun and the rush of wind and the endless skies. Men and women come to sleep in its velvety, dappled shade and dream visions of running water and soft, dark loam and home. Even in the depths of winter, so thick and established has its network of branches and foliage become that there is shelter for any traveler, man or beast—a haven for any who should wearily pass by.

And the years turn—and it has been here forever, established and deep-rooted. Its branches touch the vault of the sky, brushing the stars lightly and caressing the moon as she swings past. Its roots reach into the earth to wrap around the pulsing beat that trembles in the darkness of the deeps.

And then with a fickle turn, as easily as she graced this tree with manifold blessings, Nature rescinds her gift. She throws a terrible spear from the heavens. What has taken centuries to coax forth from a tiny seed is destroyed in an instant, in a deadly arc of blindingly beautiful, blazing lightning.

It sunders.

It sears white-hot.

It shatters to splinters.

The earth shudders at the tremors of the blow.

Meaning: Catastrophe, sudden change, crisis, releasing all emotion, suffering a blow to the ego, revelation, and seeing through illusions. A necessary disruption to the status quo—violent and explosive upheaval as the only way to break through the long-established patterns. Fantasies shattered by the harsh and brutal hand of reality. Making a clean and utter severing from the past. It is time to re-examine belief structures and opinions.

XVII The Star

$\mathcal{S}$ILVER GILDED FOOTSTEPS glide on silver flowing streams with the silver glowing starlight etching night in silver seams.

There is no sun. There is no moon. In the hushed stillness of the blackest night, only a trail of stars glitters like a fortune in diamonds upon the velvet carpet of the sky. The river of the Milky Way pours across the heavens in a cascade of starry pinpricks, and she comes dancing down that lane to where the celestial river runs to the silver-etched earthly waters.

Water and earth and air become a single element in her presence. Walk on one, swim through the other, it matters not which; they are as she wills them to be.

She dances, and her feet are so light, there is but the barest disturbance of ripples upon her watery dance floor. She dances the dance that the stars have choreographed in their millennia of gazing down on the earth. It is their silent homage to the burning spirit they have witnessed. It is the dance and flow of human life, condensed into a pure essence of painful beauty. It is Hope made into a visual form.

She stretches and strains, sways and arches, leaps to impossible heights in time to a tempo that beats in the silent pulses of the stars above. A cascade of river droplets sprays forth from her swirling form. Where each droplet falls, a flowery tendril slowly sprouts.

She dances tirelessly through the night, inhuman and yet embodying humanity in her very being. When the glow of dawn touches the eastern sky, she clasps her silvery cloak tight. There is a sudden weariness to her eyes, but it is edged with triumph as well. She steps up the slowly furling carpet of the Milky Way, back to her sister stars in the night, where they gleam and wait for the next true night to dance again.

Meaning: Regaining hope, faith in the future, inspiration. Finding the still and silent place within your being of serenity, tranquility amid trouble, harmony, offering without reservations, sharing and being generous. The harshness of daylight or even moonlight is gone, and there is nothing but the calm and nonjudgmental eyes of the stars. There is a peace to that, a space to gather up, prepare, and uplift the spirit. Let loose doubts and fears to the embrace of the night. The stars have always been symbols of guidance and hope, the light to lead you home. A resilient fish, carp symbolize strength, perseverance, courage, and determination of spirit. The chrysanthemums, commonly representative of longevity, are also symbols of hope.

You demi-puppets that by moonshine do the green sour ringlets make, whereof the ewe not bites, and you whose pastime is to make midnight mushrooms ...

—Shakespeare, *The Tempest* (Act V, Scene I)

XVIII The Moon

$\mathcal{T}$HE WATCHFUL EYE of the sun has closed, and the harshness that day shines upon the world is blurred and erased. The moon rises upon this, her domain, to spy on those of the half-world who begin to creep forth. A mushroom faery ring glows bright in those soft, silvery waves. As the moments pass and the gloam closes in, they glow brighter and brighter with their own phosphorescence to light the path for the faery queen.

"She comes hither!" cry the sprites on the wind, with voices so lovely they drive mortals mad with longing. "Make way!" call the will-o'-the-wisps, darting through the woods. They spark and glitter to taunt and lead astray any human who might be passing, but there is no human toy for them to catch hold of tonight. The dryads clasp hands from among the gray birches and shed their leaves as they step forward lightly to be handmaids to the approaching queen. As she glides through the forest, anemones spring up beneath her bare feet, and she smiles as she begins the dancing.

Make way! Make way!
The night holds sway;
lead on the dance to fend off day!
With mad delight, come hear us sing:
no sorrow here, no pond'rous thought,
no secrets held, no secrets sought,
for all that's wrought in faery's ring
is wild abandon.
Let sense take wing!

Meaning: Fears and anxieties, believing illusions, experiencing distortion, chasing after fantasy, dreams and visions, disorientation. The fey are masterful at the arts of illusion, and the dangers of stepping into a mushroom faery ring are well known. The Moon is the realm beyond the known and comfortable and predictable. It is the otherworld, awesome and inspiring in its own right, and daunting and dangerous if ill-respected. It is easy to be the wayward traveler who is distracted by will-o'-the-wisps and led astray to be lost, wandering, in the woods; but if one keeps the wits about, a glimpse beyond the bounds of sunlit reality is the rarest honor and most inspiring of enchantments. It is a doorway to hidden unknowns, and the wellspring of mingled dark and light that seeps forth from there. That is the gift of the Moon.

XIX The Sun

$\mathcal{I}$N A FLARE of liquid gold that pours across the sky, the sun rises. It is the brilliant star of day, banishing the thin and wispy light of his night-bound siblings in the rich glow of dawn.

The King of the Birds emerges from his slumbering roost as the morning mist rises in hazy waves from the dew-dampened ground. His feathers gleam iridescent under dawn's rosy palette of warmth-tinged light. His companion mounts, and together they set wing across the lands of their domain. They glide across the valleys, hearing the songs rise from workers in the fields. They soar up high and taunt the mountaintops with an elusive brush of wingtips across the upper peaks.

The denizens of the day trail in an entourage of avian delight. They pour across the sky, trailing after the sun in the arc of its journey to the western horizon.

From fallow field and verdant vale,
from sun-bleached shores with diamond grains,
and moonlit trails that trek like veins
through mountain, river, past the end
where sky is but a ghostly veil
that to Beyond transcends ...

I summon all the winged kin
from this horizon to the bounds
of what is dreamt and all surrounds!
The voices of forbidden songs
will spiral through and center in
to fall where they belong!

Meaning: Enlightenment and understanding, glory, achieving prominence. The constant renewal of life, vitality, filled with radiant joy and energy, invigoration, and good health. Being full of assurance and confidence, a clarity of vision and purpose lit by the clear daylight. From the times of ancient civilizations up to the present, the sun has always been a symbol of life and growth. It has been embodied in vibrant gods and goddesses in cultures throughout the ages—young and glorious and brilliant, full of vigor and blazing splendor. The strength and power of the gods pours forth in the nourishing glow of the sun.

XX Judgement

$\mathcal{U}$PON THE ARRIVAL of Judgment Day, an angel sounds the horn to send out the Blast of Truth. Let all the souls rise to that call then and lay their deeds out to be seen and judged by all. Let the spirit be cleansed with burning light and fire, to be made pure.

There comes a time for everyone when an accounting must be held. It is time to evaluate the phase of life just past, to recognize and to appraise with an unbiased mind and honesty to oneself. Every action has its result, for good or for ill, to be rewarded or to bear the need for absolution and forgiveness, cleansing and atonement. And beyond that is the transition on to the next phase, a rebirth and a clean slate to begin again.

Red poppies are a symbol of sleep and death, sometimes as an offering for the dead. Like blood, their color stains the fields, brilliant and beautiful. From that life-filled expanse of delicately swaying crimson and gold, butterflies take wing to bear the spirits onward in the metamorphosis of the soul. The wide freedom and endless blue of the beyond awaits.

Meaning: Release and renewal, absolution, the freshness of a new dawn, a new start. Making a judgment, though it might be harsh and difficult to face; the necessity of hard choices. Face down those decisions, recognize the need, and forgive. Reawakening, the mystery of birth and death. The voice of destiny summons you onward. Hearing that undeniable call and being drawn to act upon it; knowing what must be done.

XXI The World

$\mathcal{T}$HE PULSE OF the World ripples in an affirmation of all the life that it holds and all the death that passes. Every leaf and tree, every creature—from the smallest insects to the great singing whales—the patterns that they weave as they are born and die and cycle onward, all tremble in unison with that single heartbeat, brought together by a mighty conductor. It is a wonderfully discordant harmony, the essence of balance, a unity of disparate parts.

She sets the crown of insight lightly on her brow. She wears the girdle of truth. She reaches within and feels the lifeline that she is connected to as well. She touches it, and it is like a tangible presence in her heart, delicate but strong. The shining web of connections stretches from her heart and out into the ether. And then she reaches out with her mind, above, so high! She feels at one with the soaring birds, knows the stretch and strain of wing muscles flexing and balancing on the wind, knows the kiss of sunlight on her outstretched leaves and branches, feels the slow erosion of water on stone over the millennia.

There is no past or present or later, for this heartbeat has pulsed from the first spark of the universe, and it will beat until the end of time. It is an everlasting moment of Now, and the shimmering web of connection thrums gloriously hot in her veins. With a sudden clarity, she knows in that instant that she is blessed.

Meaning: Satisfaction and peace of mind. A successful conclusion, and the end is in sight. Achieving balance, melding and blending to bring together in unison the multiple songs of life. The World is a card of realized goals and prosperity. It is a state of completion, though not without a share of involvement and hard work to attain. When one's goals have been reached, there is a space, a quiet breath of a moment in time when a feeling of ultimate fulfillment spills through the consciousness. It is a wondrous and precious moment, the culmination of hard work, to see your dreams come true and to know that elusively mythical treasure promised in fairy tales: the heart's desire.

Wands

Wands are the suit of the fire element.

Ace

T is the possibility of creativity, excitement, adventure; a challenge to step forward with courage and confidence.

Plant the wand firmly in the ground and see it blaze forth with crimson light. Like a response of flint striking tinder, inspiration blooms from that illumination. The spirits and sylphs are drawn forth from their dwellings. In ordinary light they hide, indistinguishable from leaf and twig and stone and sky, but in this glow they slip out and stretch their wings. They sense that something is beginning. A spark has been lit. A challenge has been whispered. An invitation has been extended in this dawn hour.

Once lit, fire is unpredictable and difficult to control. Uncontained energy can flare into a raging wildfire. Seize this wild opportunity, and glory in the blaze.

They are beings of fire and the guardians for the wands: foxes, cats, lions. They flash with the sparks of intellect and wit, with fleet bodies that dart through the world, and with the burning flame of a fierce and strong spirit.

Two

SHE SURVEYS THE lands that lie before her. This is her domain. It is filled with her subjects, and she has ruled over all that the eye can see from this high vantage point, as have her ancestors before her. For a moment, her sight hazes, and she sees a vision of what she might accomplish in the years to come, having been granted this power. At last, this is the chance to bring her dreams to fruition and to build the reality that she long has envisioned for these lands. She knows she must grasp the reins of power tightly. She must be bold and certain and unwavering in the path that she etches for her people, for there are those who would be swift to pounce and take her place should weakness be detected.

Her companion, the lion, knows his place as king of the beasts. He embodies courage and authority. From the pinnacle, he boldly stares down any who dare to challenge the two of them. He lifts his mighty head, shakes back the fiery, crackling mane, and his roar rings out across the valley as if to mark the farthest edges of their dominion with the reach of his voice.

The Two of Wands is the emblem of personal power and influence, authority, and courage. Now is the time to be bold and inventive, and not to shy away from doing what is necessary. But also beware of letting the intoxication of power cloud the mind and judgment.

Three

*T*HIS IS THE bridge that stretches to
the edge of the world. Its lower steps beckon for
the brave and the curious to step up and begin
that trek. It arcs out across the sky ... but then
it goes no further. She stands there upon the edge and wonders
where to go from here. The sun dazzles the eyes from above and
shines in a shimmering ribbon of light along the river that etches
out the canyon so far below. There is a crystalline, timeless quality
to the air this high up. It is charged with static that sparks like all
the potential she knows is waiting for her here and waiting inside
her. Each breath chills and exhilarates.

She sees the wands of those who have come this far before
her, and perhaps from here they turned back, daunted by what
the next step may be. She pauses a moment, does not look down,
and then steps forward into what seems to be empty space. She
feels sturdy rock and shale materialize under her feet. She realizes
then that this entire bridge has been built by the steps and the
dreams of others. She takes a breath and then begins to make her
own strides—she takes the next step, and the next, and the bridge
begins to grow beneath her feet.

The Three of Wands invites you to explore, seek out the
uncharted, expand your horizons. Take a long view of situations,
and express leadership.

Four

SPRING HAS ARRIVED, and the flowers are in bloom! The roses send forth their sweet scent as an invitation to the dwellers of the fey realms. The ground trembles as the unicorns of the east, the *kierun*, spring forward to heed the call and lead the faery hosts on this ride of celebration. The chill has left the air, but this respite is but a moment to enjoy, and then the greater work must begin afterwards. Until then, this time must be made the most of.

The heralds lift up their trumpets, and the clarion call echoes out to the dawn. The wind tangles in manes and wings, and trails in their wake. Faster and faster they ride, until the world is a blur of color, and then, with a cry of jubilation, they spring up into the air and ride across the skies.

The Four of Wands calls for celebration. Initial successes have brought hope and joy to the air. There is harmony and peace to be had. However, once attained, this prosperity must be maintained as well. Take a moment to breathe and enjoy, but be prepared to continue with the work that has achieved this point. The fire must remain lit. It must be fed constantly to keep the blaze going and not be allowed to die out to embers. Let go of limitations, and embrace the freedom being offered.

Five

AT THE FOREFRONT of the pack, the hare sprints away. It darts past rocks and trees, slips under branches. Its paws flash across the ground with the race of adrenaline in its veins—the red, living pulse of blood that his pursuers scent. It drives them to a frenzy as they race after that elusive and pale streak. They race against each other, nearly climbing upon each other's backs in their efforts of chase, leaping from the tops of the wands, springing wildly through the air. Everyone for himself!

And through the battle of fiery brindled fur, he charges. They do all they can to obstruct him, as if for the mere enjoyment of conflict. It is like swimming upstream against a powerful surge. Exhaustion burns in the muscles and the lungs. At times there is a thin voice from within that urges, "Just lie down. Let the tide of strife wash over and past." But no, to do so would be to be trampled beneath the onrush. He does not falter. He feels his own pulse heat up with the excitement of this strife. It is an uphill struggle of living obstacles that he wades through. He feels a bit like the hare himself, struggling to break through to get to his haven. In the Five of Wands, sometimes it seems the world tosses dozens of obstacles in your path. When gathered together, these minor obstructions become an overwhelming wall to overcome, but take heart and let the adrenaline awaken body and mind to rise to the challenge. Answer that challenge not with despair but with renewed vigor. Appreciate the unknown strengths that are drawn forth when faced with difficulties.

Six

$\mathcal{H}$E STANDS UPON the stone lion, symbol of kings and emperors, and proclaims his ascendancy with a triumphant declaration. Even the lion bows his head and closes his jaws to this victor. It lies quiescent and submissive.

He bears his wand like a scepter and raises aloft the laurel crown. He knows his star is rising, and he dares any to challenge him. He has seen many challengers come and go—brave knights and foolish knights. The clever ones who thought to outwit him, the famed ones with their followers, and those who were full of bravado but little skill. None have yet been able to best him.

He is confident in his own strength and abilities, prideful and arrogant, certain that there is no one equal to his might. And yet, he reached this position by fighting through the masses and distinguishing himself—perhaps the one challenger who will beat him eventually is still waiting in the wings for his own time, waiting for the right moment to strike to take down this overly confident king.

The Six of Wands symbolizes victory and triumph. One has prevailed and overcome many obstacles to come out on top. But you must beware falling prey to hubris and lassitude that uncontested victory may bring, and not become lost in self-importance.

Seven

*T*HE VIXEN FACES off against a badger, while her kits watch from beneath the protective curl of her tail. The enemies circle and circle. They size each other up. A nip here to test the swiftness of reaction; a swipe to press the defenses. The vixen snarls and lunges forward, for she has her brood to protect, and she will not fail them! Fear for her kits burns in her heart. Her actions are necessity, not merely courage, and yet it is all the more courageous for being such a selfless act, without the tangle of thoughts and justifications. Her mere belief makes her fight ten times more fiercely and with a fiery strength.

The bamboo of the wands signifies strength and fortitude. Bamboo possesses a slender suppleness that sways in the winds and does not break. It grows tenaciously and sends out multitudinous shoots in all directions, the better to compete for sun and space.

The Seven of Wands represents taking a stand, defending what you believe in. The world is full of strife and stiff competition, and one must have courage in facing the difficulties that come. Do not buckle under a stiff wind, but sway like the bamboo. Seemingly insurmountable odds can be overcome with faith and courage.

Eight

S HE SETS HER staff before her, step by step to the top of the rise. The glow-globes wave lacy fronds on either side of the path. She remembers how a childhood friend called them wishes, and that to take one and blow myriad seeds to the wind would send that wish out. And the farther those seedlings traveled, the more power for truth and fulfillment they would gain.

She bends down to pluck one. With the puff of a breath, she sends the seedlings on their way. It is the ending of the lovely flower that blooms so delicately into elaborate spheres of ethereal beauty, but the beginning of a new growth. The seeds spin away on the wild winds—at the mercy of entropy but sailing with the purpose nature bestowed on them with the gift of gossamer filaments. Sail away and beyond, and then set down to grow to become a mighty tree!

The Eight of Wands is the beginning of a long journey towards a goal. A great undertaking is at hand, and it speeds towards reward with hope and momentum.

Nine

THE SENTINELS KEEP watch from above, ever wary, ever vigilant. They are the eternal guardians. They defend against the unknowns that lie hidden in the abyss—perhaps it is just light and mist and the edge of the world, but they have not yet ventured beyond to see with their own eyes. They know only that they have been charged to watch, gaze glued to the west, from where the light fades each dying day.

When the last rays shoot forth and the green flash bids the sun farewell, what will come from night's abyss? Can their forces withstand the assault? They have not yet been tested. Each day when the dusk fades to black, they wait for their unnamed foe and strain their eyes to the western darkness and wonder if this will be the night he comes. It is easy to be proud, tall, and at attention when the strength of the sun shines upon their shoulders. It is much harder to keep that through the silence of the twilight hours. And yet, they hold true, for they know one day they will be needed.

Vigilance is the watchword for the Nine of Wands. It urges you to keep strength in reserve and to always be prepared for any eventuality. Retain a core of power; even more importantly, know what that inner strength is, for sometimes we possess an ability to endure through travails that is not evident until put to the test. It is easy, though, to become lax and to lose the edge when the challenge does not rise as quickly or as often as expected. Maintaining that acuity can be the most difficult challenge of all.

Ten

$\mathcal{T}$HIS DRYAD BEARS the weight of what seems to be a miniature world upon her back. Her branches are weighted down, bent beneath the heavy structures. The support and welfare of the beings who inhabit those towers are hers to nourish with the flow of life's sap through her branches and leaves. Their souls are the songs that spiral up through the foliage from her heart. But the gray cold seeps into her roots, and it is a hard burden to bear. She pushes and strains upwards, reaches towards the sun for that fire that can help to sustain through dark times.

The fires of the wands are burning low, and it may seem that there are only embers left from the great roaring furnace that was. So many demands and dependencies! She struggles and tries to keep her head uplifted, to hold to that center of creativity and nourishment.

Overextending, taking on far too much, burdened with overwhelming responsibility, being held accountable, doing things the hard way. Perhaps those little beings who live among her branches do not need the constant watchfulness and nourishment that she believes must be her duty. And yet it is given freely, the burden is taken on willingly, and she knows she has the strength within to bear it and flourish.

Page

Music is the universal language of mankind.
—Henry Wadsworth Longfellow

*W*ITH CONFIDENCE AND a child-like joy, she plays her instrument, sending forth her message. The cadences dance in swirling melodies, a song of confidence and assurance. The strident beats mark a quick tempo that is irresistible to any who hear it. She smiles, knowing that she is the center of attention as she draws out all the creatures of the woods. Excitement fills the air, and breathless exuberance.

> *From ether and the nether-realms,*
> *from sea and skies, come to my side!*
> *I summon all to heed this call:*
> *come flock to me! Come run, swim, stride!*

The Page of Wands is creative and passionate. She is witty, charismatic, and outspoken with her philosophy. She knows her mind and is direct and forthright when she has an opinion. She may be a teacher, eager to pass on that kernel of knowledge that she possesses. She is the fiery spark of initiative, inventive, and she dares you to delve within and seek out the opportunities that may be frightening but have so much potential. Sometimes the actions that push you to the limits of comfort are the most rewarding. She tells you to do and not sit there with only mute desire. Action is what is important. Can you hear her song ringing in your ears? Can you hear its sweet seduction singing with the voice of impulse?

Knight

$\mathcal{T}$HE KNIGHT OF Wands indicates change and progression towards a goal. He is an individual full of daring and passion. His spirit is ablaze with the fire that the wands suit symbolizes, and like fire, the bright, brindled fur of his lion mount and his fox attendants flash through the woods as they dart in a flaming entourage through the trees. The wind runs rippling fingers through his hair, and he laughs for the joy of that sensation and the power leashed in the muscles of the lion, bunching and stretching beneath him.

This knight is on a journey for adventure. Excitement flows along in his trail. He does not necessarily seek it, but his presence invariably spurs rivalry and conflict, perhaps because of his cocky and assured attitude and self-confidence. Sometimes his aggressive nature can be seen as being overconfident, too impetuous.

He is a knight with a blazing lion's heart and the sparking cleverness of foxes, though not always the wisdom to match it. He recklessly rides crashing through the world, leaping from cliffs in heroic bounds towards his destination. Such a wondrously heroic sight to glimpse him as he passes! Destiny, faith, and the purity of his goal shine with an effervescent glow in his eyes, so that perhaps he does not notice the flowers he may trample along the path in his headlong plunge. Be wary of allowing the wild temper and flaming energy of this knight to cause discord and interruption.

Queen

*T*HE FIRE-BRINDLED FUR of foxes darting about in the shadows surrounds her. They watch among the other denizens of the forest who are drawn out by the singing of the harp on which the queen plays. She glows in the midday light, her presence like a white-hot flame that radiates with the warmth of her spirit. The Queen of Wands' fingers dance across the strings, and she embraces the tree that is at once her audience of dryads, her instrument, and her living wand.

The Queen of Wands is dedicated, engaging, and attractive. She is always cheerful and upbeat. She knows the role of a queen and plays it with perfect, calm assurance. She is used to being the center of attention and knows it is her due. Her presence exudes confidence and the knowledge that she can handle anything and anyone. It is not arrogance but a simple understanding and truthful assessment of her skills and abilities. It is easy for her charms to be turned towards darker purposes of deceit and manipulation. She guards against this temptation.

Mesmerized by this, the world hushes at her entrance to hear her, see her, and bathe in her radiance. Her exuberance in life sings out as her hands dance across trills and runs and glissandos upon the living harp.

King

HE HOLDS HIS staff aloft like a torch, a beacon of flame and light. Or perhaps he himself is that beacon, gleaming as he does with the fire that burns within his chest and as a searing crown upon his brow. He lifts up the fiery torch to illuminate the path and strides forward. The ground shifts, and the denizens of the woods step back. The trees part before him, lifting their branches to make way for his passage. The environment shifts to his will and obeys his unspoken desires and commands.

The King of Wands is charismatic. The force of his charm is irresistible, such that the very world seems to mold to his desires and bow to his will. He is a source of inspiration and bears his mantle of authority with an ease, as if he were born to it. It is his natural element, burning bright within him—blazing in his blood, in his voice, and searing all that his gaze touches.

He has the spirit of the lion within him: proud and fierce, dominant, and unafraid to chase down what he desires. He springs forth into action with the confidence, strength, and lithe grace of that great beast. He is bold and does not balk at taking chances or striking out upon new, risky paths.

Cups

Cups are the suit of the water element.

Ace

I T IS THE initial drop of water that falls upon the glass-smooth surface of a lake. There is an almost imperceptible ripple that starts to spread in expanding rings. It is the shrug of a tiny earthquake that sends a shudder up through ocean waters to culminate in crashing waves upon a distant shore. It is the first stirring of emotion, of compassion and love, of intimacy, and of attunement—this tiny drop of potential that will join into a river of all the other mingled droplets from humanity. They all trickle together to flow into one vast sea of swirling emotions.

The still surface of the water in the suit of cups is like a scrying mirror. Delve into those crystalline depths, heed the twinges of intuition, and then raise the glass and drink deeply. This grail shines with a light of understanding and inner knowledge.

These are the guardians of the cups: the denizens of the deep, the fish and the ancient spirits of the sea. They swim with a fluid grace through the ocean's depths, living in a dance of eternal motion. The waxing and waning of the moon pulls the tides and currents of the sea to swell and ebb, and this rhythm is felt thrumming through the blood of all who dwell in the ocean's embrace.

Two

*T*HIS IS THE melding of water and earth and air, the alchemy of elements. Golden as the goblets, the fish swim through the waters (or is it air that they glide through?). The dryads coil around each other, braided into an embrace as fluid as the air (or is it the sea?) that they are surrounded by. They are soulmates. They twist together to form one solid trunk, and yet they retain their individuality and their own colors.

Like the harmonious swirl of a yin-yang, they circle one another in a liquid push and pull that unifies. They share a cup. "Drink," one whispers, proffering the goblet.

"I accept," one responds, and takes it into her hands. They drink deeply, at once, and the shared sap flows down into their roots.

The other cup balances precariously on an outstretched branch. They do not seem to notice it, though the spirits and sylphs watch it carefully. For now it stands stable, but as the trees grow, as the branches stretch and uncoil and burst into bloom, will that cup still stand upright or will it tip and tumble to the ground, spilling its precious liquid?

The Two of Cups is about making a connection, a union, a partnership. It is the bringing together of opposites and the potential for bonding. It is a relationship. Like a living organism, relationships grow; the ones that are strong become pillars of stability, and the weak connections are gradually forgotten and fall apart.

Three

THERE IS A song that dwells at the ocean's floor. It lurks in the chasms. It hides in the voices of whales and the squeals of dolphins. It haunts the reefs and caverns. And then, once in a great while, like an air bubble that has been gathering under the crust, it bursts forth in an unstoppable swell to rise towards the surface.

The sirens of the deep have been waiting for this moment. They come together when they feel the signal that trembles through the waves to all the corners of the sea. They sing. Their voices weave a countermelody and descant to the ocean's song. Laughter rings in trills and glissandos that send ripples from their lips. That gleeful shudder of the waters summons the denizens of the sea, all the varied creatures among the ocean swells, to follow in the wake of the sirens.

The very movement of all the beings who swim through the waters is an elegant dance of undulation, a powerful slicing through the waves. The liquid dance of the sea bursts to the surface, and the song echoes to the vast vault of the heavens.

The Three of Cups is a call to celebration, dancing, and singing. Friendship is its key component, and companionship, relying on others, and developing community and team spirit.

Four

SHE MAKES HER way to the surface. The water's surface shivers at her approach, and then she bursts through that barrier to climb up on the rocks. The water streams from her hair and shoulders. She flicks an arc of shining droplets off her tail. Like diamonds, the spray sparkles in the air, then vanishes beneath the surface.

She lies there, still and holding her breath until she is certain that no one has followed her. Who would? They only have eyes and mind and sense for the world beneath the waves. But she waits anyway. She wants to be certain she is alone. She is bored of them, tired of the existence of the endless dance of the sea.

The ripples of her disruption smooth away, and soon the water's surface becomes a glassy mirror. The blue of sky melts into the reflected blue of water in a seamless gradation of color and light. Her mind escapes for a moment in dreamy contemplation. She sees her reflection for the first time. She is struck by her own beauty, not in a vain way, but with the fascination of discovery. She gazes into the reflected eyes that seem like tiny pools of water in themselves. She reaches out to touch that creature who gazes back at her. With a sudden shock, her fingers meet the glass and the image is shattered into a dozen ripples.

She startles, and only then becomes aware that she is not as alone as she first thought. Though the sea denizens have left her to her own devices, the sylphs of the air have crept close during her distraction, and they watch her intently, amused, mocking. Suddenly the air feels chill upon her drying skin, and she yearns for the soothing embrace of the sea and her kin.

The Four of Cups represents self-absorption, introspection, sinking too deeply into one's own concerns and being lost in reveries. Awareness of anything else fades, and the world seems gray. But the outside world has much to offer if you tear your gaze away from your own reflection.

Five

SHE TREKS ACROSS the sand dunes. Her feet sink in with each step, so that her legs ache by the time she reaches the water's edge. She walks to the end of the strand, clasping the half-filled (half-empty?) bowl tightly, afraid it'll slip from her numb fingers and shatter on the rocky shore.

The water is icy at her feet. The surf laps at her toes, bringing a chill that eats into her bones. It makes her body feel brittle. She shivers. She thinks it is the wind brushing her shoulder but does not notice that it is instead the sprites. They brush her hair back with gentle fingers and whisper comfort in her ears, but she hardly notices, so intent is she upon her own sorrows and woes.

She has sent her hopes out across the sea. They have set sail upon a white ship, and she wonders when and if they will return, fulfilled.

She fills the bowl with her tears, taking an almost sensual delight in the slide of those droplets down her cheeks. She imagines a fish swimming through those tears, swimming through the air of the empty bowl, unbound by liquid or air. And then she sets that briny offering next to the others on the ground.

The Five of Cups wallows in regret and loss. It is rejection of pleasure, feeling sorrow, and wishing for what might have been.

Six

SHE WANDERS ALONG the path until she comes to her destination. The creek burbles along its bed not far below her chosen spot, and she sets up her table and teacups to receive her visitors—first her friends from home, with their shiny button eyes and thread-sewn smiles.

And then the shyer ones begin to creep forth from the shadows and hollows of the woods: the sylphs and nymphs from the glassy water below, the dryads from the birch and beech and oak, and the goblins from under. These are the companions she has been waiting for, and she greets them cheerfully. They are drawn forth by her innocent chatter and by the mind that has not yet been chained by boundaries of "what must be" and definitions of impossibility. In her world, fish are not bound by the water of the creek—they may swim through the air above that glassy path—and the sylvan company she entertains at her table are as welcome as the ones made of cloth and stuffing.

The Queen of the Faeries steps forth, and the fantastic retinue draws back, but the girl just smiles, pours a cup of tea, and offers it with a smile.

The Six of Cups is a reminder of childhood innocence, good intentions, noble impulses, simple joys and pleasures. It is not meant to be overly sentimental, but more an urging to remember the open-mindedness of a child's perspective, and to push back the narrowness that folds in on you over time, with the complexities of life and responsibility.

Seven

ER HEAD IS lost in the clouds. She has stars in her eyes, and her mental focus is occluded by the moon as she looks to the castle in the sky. She is mentally and physically ungrounded and unaware of their precarious perch. In her eagerness, she might take an unwary step and plummet from that high perch into the misty abyss that surrounds them. The winds whip at her hair and clothing in a turmoil of excitement.

Meanwhile, he is a little more grounded. While she gazes to the vision of the floating dream, his eyes are on the castles that are on the surrounding cliff sides. Though difficult to reach, they are attainable, even though the arcane symbols on his map may be obscure. He knows the pain of yearning for the impossible.

But she doesn't. "Look up!" she says. Her fingers linger on his shoulder as she urges him to listen to her desire and see. He nods absently. He tries to ignore the thoughts of "What if we could reach the floating citadel...?" and continues to scrutinize the map that the Magician gave to him.

The Seven of Cups involves indulging in fantasies. You have too many options to choose from. With so many paths, that task becomes daunting. There are too many desires. Some of them are within the realm of reality, others... not so much. Some are wise courses of actions, others merely sing with the siren song of temptation that could lead to a destructive path. There are unlimited possibilities.

Eight

SEEKER OF THE seas, dive down, dive deep. Plumb the sapphire waters so dark that they pulse with the nacreous gleam of black pearls. Slice through the waters, O seeker of truth; slide with lithe body through the currents and undertows; turn away from the sunlight of the world up above that blinds with its too-sharp brilliance. Like the delicate luminescence of the deep sea life, there are some things that can only be seen when the eyes are enlarged in the dim, nether-lit otherworld. Dive down, seeker of the seas!

The Eight of Cups beckons you to follow and delve within for personal discovery and answers. Turn away and disengage from the material world for the spiritual. Leave the sharp lines and edges, the harsh sounds that pierce the dry air with a clarion call. The sea's embrace is much softer and more sensual, and connected by the ripples and the flows. The water softens the assaults on the senses, so that everything becomes fluid and smooth.

The Eight of Cups shimmers with the distant touch of the sun's rays from above. They tumble down into the depths. The falling glimmer and shine urges you to move on to catch hold of one of them. Now is the time to let go and allow all the weariness to ripple away from you and fade into the waves.

Nine

$\mathcal{A}$LL THAT THE heart desires is within reach, just at his fingertips, swirling like the rich, golden tones of the massive school of fish. They tumble and slice through the waves in a frenetic arc and spasm of exuberance, until the mass of bodies seems to squeeze even water out from the space.

There is a sensual delight in the sleek forms brushing past his skin. They sing with a joy of life and the abundance to be found for the taking to those who reach out. The world extends an offering of pleasure, intoxicating in its beauty. There is a grace in the swirl of fish as they swim in unison and spin through the water as one organic being, rather than as hundreds of disparate creatures. They swim with such harmony that it feels like a choreographed dance.

Fish are symbolic of health, prosperity, and good fortune. The Nine of Cups entices with the pleasure of the senses, satisfaction, and wish fulfillment. The future is assured, and there is bounty on the horizon.

Ten

*T*HE WATER SWIRLS around the two of them. The wavetops have been kissed by the sun, and the waters are warm and inviting. They drift in that fluid embrace, buoyed by a lightness that flares in their hearts. Like twin mini-suns, caught in each other's gravity, they orbit around each other. The world outside ceases to exist with this attainment of heart's desire. They want for nothing. They need no others to make this moment complete, but there is a union nevertheless between the two of them and all the surrounding living creatures.

The school of fish sends a maelstrom of bubbles to froth in a dizzy swirl around their entangled limbs. Their joy radiates outward in a luminous shelter of protection. Fish are symbols of plenty and prosperity. They slice through the azure depths, and their scales sparkle like glimmers of living gold. This moment of bliss, of seemingly eternal and final contentment, is real, but it must be nurtured and nourished, else it can easily slip back away into the depths of the ocean, like a scattered school of fish.

The Ten of Cups is the final attainment of serenity and peace. Success and happiness have been granted at last—an all-encompassing emotional contentment, not just a physical or material pleasure. Family support and bonds are important to being able to enjoy the blessings of life.

Page

SHE DELVES DOWN through the waves, seeking to be alone and to find a peaceful place to contemplate her own thoughts.

She brings a cup with her. It brims with the captured essence of sunlight from the world so high above her own. It contains the tiny sparks and flashes that have drifted down to the sea bed in bits of golden coin or in the stray shaft of sunlight that manages to pierce through the fathoms. All of that is distilled into the precious contents held in her hands.

She lifts the cup underneath her face, feels that remembered warmth of the sun's kiss upon the wavetops. The heat spirals out through the water with tendrils of peace and tranquility. The radiance sparks her thoughts and her imagination. She feels her mind begin to set adrift, and her vision fills with dreams of the fantastic.

The Page of Cups is sentimental. She is a true romantic at heart, and in a world that is filled with so much noise and bustle, she longs for the time and space to simply breathe and to truly take in the pleasures that abound. She listens to the still voice from deep inside that speaks with understanding and intuition, and she longs to believe in the impossible.

Knight

*T*HE UNICORN IS a child of the sea, born of foam and restless waves, surging with the wild abandon of the surf. Only those with purity of heart may lay a hand upon such a creature, much less ride upon her back. The Knight of Cups is her companion on the eternal quest. The two of them are alone on this mystical journey.

He is the knight of the Round Table on the grand quest for the Grail. He is the romantic who seeks where his heart and emotions lead. He is the artist and the musician and the poet whose eyes see into the unseen nether-realms of imagination. He is the idealist who will not let mere physical laws stop him from riding with reckless abandon across the wavetops on his journey.

The Knight of Cups follows his dreams. He lets his intuition guide him on his journeys. Sea sprites and foamy sylphs tell him of the wonders far beyond the explored lands, and he yearns to follow those spirits and see with his own eyes. The golden grail embodies the perfection he yearns for. He knows if he remains honest and faithful, and follows the truths that his heart speaks, that he can one day taste from that cup.

The waves churn in his wake, and he does not know nor care what lurks below the sapphire waves; he sees only the beauty that sparkles in the spraying droplets.

Queen

*T*HE VERY BEING of the Queen of Cups is a creative nexus. She is poetry in motion, imagination incarnate. She can dance upon the swells of the ever-shifting, ever-changing seas in unison with the dance of life that engages all of the world and its creatures around her.

She heeds her intuitions and follows her heart. She listens to the whispers of the stars, for she knows they are much wiser than any being on this earth. They have witnessed the world from when the seas were young.

Though her steps seem random and impulsive, she relies upon a deep-seated knowledge. She draws her strength from the vast abyss of the ocean. The ancients of the deeps, the sea turtles, the wise ones of the ocean: they come swimming up to join her in a joyous celebration. The world that they jointly move in is like a dream. Everything is fluid, one element melding into the next. It is the shifting landscape of the subconscious, overlapping with the material being of reality. This is the essence of creation and artistic expression.

Guided by instincts, she is attuned to that otherworld and finds joy in that communion of kindred spirits. For someone else who did possess a comprehension of her synchronicity, a misstep from her position would mean a plunge into unfathomable depths, but not so for the Queen of Cups. She dances on, embraced by the endless azure ocean and heavens, and where the sea meets the sky, there is no seam.

King

$\mathcal{H}$E IS WISE and understanding. He knows the meaning of patience. Like the sea turtles that swim at his side, he guides the way with a steady calm through the ever-shifting uncertainties of the vast ocean depths. He reads the knowledge of the centuries that has been etched into the patterns on their shells, and drinks in that gift with every breath taken of the water that flows in and around them all. The waters grow still and peaceful in his presence. The cerulean swells sparkle with a gemlike clarity.

The sea horse is a symbol of the power of Poseidon and is imbued with the tireless strength of the sea. He is a patient creature, swimming through the swells at his own fluid pace. He follows the currents. However, his grace is armored by the spines of his exoskeleton, and that sinuous delicacy should not be underestimated, for the male sea horse is the protector of the young.

Like the sea horse, the King of Cups is a protector. He cares for and watches over all those who are near to him. He offers a drink from his healing waters. He offers compassion and care. His message is to let the currents flow through your veins to cleanse your heart of its burdens. He is patient and tolerant, and understands that all aspects and needs of the people around him must be balanced.

Swords

Swords are the suit of the air element.

Ace

$\mathcal{A}$ SWORD IS DOUBLE-EDGED. It can slice with the swift assurance of justice to clear the obstructions that hide the truth. It can be the beacon to use intelligence and fairness to achieve clarity. Or it can be wielded with the arrogance of raw power in the heat of rage. These are the two sides of the strength that is embodied in this weapon—two very different uses of force to work one's will upon the world.

Something is beginning now. The winds gather in whirling eddies to summon the guardians of the skies: the wisps and the souls and the feathered ones. From that vortex, something arises that will force the duality of the Ace of Swords to slice one way or the other.

These are the sylphs of the air, and the guardians for the swords: the winged beings of the sky. A swan is lovely—she possesses downy white feathers and a slender neck that arcs with a sinuous grace—but that delicacy is a façade that cloaks a strong body and fierce nature that is unafraid of standing up. The swan will fight to protect its own, and strong wings open to catch and ride the winds across great distances.

Two

HE STANDS IN the path, warding off those who venture near. His cloaked presence is obdurate and imposing. Steel flashes as he draws the two swords to bar the way. "Who wishes to pass?" he demands, with eyes and teeth that gleam like the reflections from the twin blades. He stands there, as hard and unyielding as the metal of the forged swords. The spirits of the woods writhe and churn in the trees around him. They draw back from that cold steel, from that icy figure.

The Two of Swords is a stalemate, an impasse. Neither side will compromise, and so no progress can be made until one chooses to step aside. It is a lock-stepped balance, a strange dance that struggles to find some grace without yielding any ground. It is a denial of truth, an avoidance of what is clear before your eyes or hiding in your heart.

"Open your eyes," urges the swan, proffering a token, a flower, a poppy that is the sleeping death that existence becomes when stubborn barriers cannot be laid aside.

"Open your heart," urges the swan, tendering the beating gem, the heart that stills when there is only the desire to take and not give.

Three

HERE, THE GRAND strength and beauty of a swan is brought down by betrayal. She mourns with blood tears for that wounding of the heart. She is far from a helpless creature—she will fight ferociously to defend herself or her young—and yet there is no sign of struggle; perhaps she bared herself as a sacrifice. She stepped forth alone and laid down her defenses. Was it anguish and grief that brought her down?

There is grief and heartbreak in the Three of Swords. There is a feeling of loneliness, separation, and isolation. There is no one to give solace or lend a hand. Has everyone deserted in this time of greatest need? The world abandons and betrays by turning its back on the destruction of beauty and the rending of a fragile emotional state.

Overcome the pain; the weeping of the heart is perhaps a necessary cleansing. Let that torment drain away; be purified of the black blood, and then lift up white wings to dance with the sky once again.

Four

HER LIMBS ARE composed in the attitude of death, but this is not that final sleep. It is just a moment of rest and recovery. Her mind floats free. She is adrift in an ether of meditation. Her eyes are closed, but she sees with another kind of vision. The sigil of an eye upon the blade she holds clasped to her chest sees down into her heart and out into the world around with a clarity that she strives for in this inner contemplation and self-imposed exile.

She floats along with the lotuses, symbols of spiritual and mental purity. Lotuses grow from the slime and muck of a lake, purified by the water to emerge in the sunlight as lovely flowers. They are a living metaphor for a seeker of spiritual truths. The pink lotus in particular is a symbol of enlightenment.

So, too, the swords that pillow her head as she meditates, as if to pierce through the fog of uncertainty and dissemble to reach a state of serenity. However, this is but a momentary rest. Her hands grip the sword tightly. She knows there are many ordeals to face still. She breathes deeply, imprints the fragrance of the lotuses in her mind. She is ready to draw the sword from the sheath and step back into a world of strife and conflict once this respite is through, though perhaps with a much clearer mental state this time.

The Four of Swords urges you to take a moment of respite. Close your eyes, and find that still and silent place at your core, where inner strength resides. Draw from that reserve in the times to come.

Five

$\mathcal{T}$HE NIGHT FADES. The rising sun pierces the sky with the blood-tinged rays of dawn, and the air is shattered by the resounding cry of the battle horn! The dark angel draws his blade to join the fray. He is accompanied by black swans. They have been steeped in the battles of self-interest and power, and they no longer gleam with the pure white of most of their brethren. Their feathers shine with the ebony luster of black pearls, a dark kind of beauty. They send raucous challenges to the heavens, relishing the oncoming conflict.

Like an arrow, he spears through the air, single-minded in his purpose. He has sacrificed his integrity to achieve his own ends, and he is focused upon himself, upon survival.

But with any conflict, there are the victorious and the defeated—one cannot exist without the other. Who is this dark angel? Is he the triumphant victor, or is he the defeated one, fleeing and cast out from his home in the heavens? The twin crossed blades on his back are reminiscent of the Two of Swords—a denial of the possibility of defeat or of the rights and wrongs of the battle that he chooses to engage in. Does the end justify the swathe he leaves in the wake of the passage of his blade?

The Five of Swords is a sign of discord and conflict of interests. The choices arrayed make it easy to profit and look to one's own concerns, for it feels the world is allied against you. Perhaps a wider view of the world might eclipse this feeling.

Six

*A*s his eyes drift shut, he feels the gentle hands that lift him onto the downy feathered back. He feels the muscular tensing of wings, the flex of sinew and bone, and then a jolt as the swan springs into the sky. His own limbs feel malleable, sapped and drained of will. She carries him high, and he curls into a fetal embrace on her back. He is content to let her bear him away.

The swan flies through the night. Her wings do not seem to tire. She does not seem to know what exhaustion is. The steady strength in the rhythmic beat of her wings and the warm, living pulse of her heartbeat beneath his own chest seem to seep through his pores and suffuse his being with a bit of her spirit. As the dawn sends tentative fingers of light into the sky, he finally cracks open his eyes to see the swiftly passing landscape far below. The land seems so distant. It is hard to believe the anguish and the fears and the tribulations that such a miniature world can create. The stormcrows caw raucously as they pass, but the sound falls upon his deaf ears. He turns his gaze forward, and as the clouds part, he can see where the swan is bearing him. He smiles and clutches tightly to her back with new strength in his fingertips.

The Six of Swords is a passage away from difficulties. It is a chance to recover after tribulations. Too much change from a bewildering world has perhaps induced despondency that you must find a way to lift out of.

Seven

*H*E HIDES HIS face behind a mask, shrouding his true nature, and he smirks in a rather satisfied way that he has managed to steal one of the swords that the swan guardian oversees. He thinks the guardian is oblivious, but she is, in fact, watching him with one eye over her shoulders. She knows and recognizes his nature.

The blackbirds descend upon him and sidle close. "What have you got there? Shiny bauble! Shiny bright!" they demand, drawn to the sullen gleam of the blade that he has taken. He turns his back to them as well, for he is the cleverest blackbird to have been able to draw this sword from the stone.

The Seven of Swords represents an attempt to escape responsibility. It is the thief who tries to make away with what is not his. He dishonorably tries to keep everything for himself and is two-faced to those who attempt to approach. The result of such an outlook on the world is uncertainty, for if one is untrustworthy, then why risk having faith in others as well? Deception breeds distrust and a pessimistic viewpoint.

Eight

*T*HE BRAMBLES CRONE lives among the blackberry hedges where the fruit is tempting and sweet, but even the leaves have wickedly curved thorns to catch and hold. The little hummingbird can navigate with ease among such treacherous tangles. She can flit through the tiny gaps and weave past the thorns with great ease. But the noble and grand elegance of the swan, with the arcing expanse of her wings, is not for such tangled and thorny corridors.

This swan is not the first to have fallen victim to the lures of the brambles crone. The old one has a collection of the skulls of those others who have thought that might and arrogant strength could overcome everything. Like the tangled enchanted briar forest that surrounded Sleeping Beauty and tempted hundreds of brave knights to die within the thorny embrace, pure might and abusive power will not always cut the path to victory.

The hummingbird flits close. "Calm," she urges, and as the swan ceases to flail, the thorns cease to cut, and the little hummingbird gently pushes one branch aside at a time, and the swan sees the light of freedom shining through from above, distant but attainable.

The Eight of Swords is a reminder not to waste energy on the trivial. It is easy to freeze up in a crisis—to feel restricted, confused, powerless, and trapped by circumstances—but there is always a way out if you take a moment to breathe and reassess.

Nine

Stormcrows herald impending dissolution
with voices cawing raucous absolution
round and round and spiraling ever near
one future sought—one future feared.

THE FUNNEL OF the sky stretches up to the heavens, an ominous tower of storms with only a tiny glimmer of hope lighting the eye of turmoil high above. "Come to me, come with me," the voice of a stormcrow whispers to him from nearby. "Let me guide you through." With anxious eyes, he gazes upwards, away, oblivious to the proffered guidance through the dark night of the soul. He clutches a sheathed sword close for security, though he could easily grasp its bright blade aloft to light the way. But he is ignorant of that beacon he holds so tight, or perhaps too weak-hearted and tremulous to wield it.

He suffers from anguish. The swords tattooed upon his breast are pinpricked markings of the regrets he experiences. He is tormented by inner fear, anxiety, guilt, and uncertainties in the night. He is a being of the air—his wings should carry him aloft, and the sky should be open and expansive and a world of freedom. Instead, it feels like a trap closing its jaws upon him with the howling winds of the approaching storm. And yet, if he were to just cast aside those doubts, he could be as free as the stormcrows that spiral in untroubled arcs above.

The Nine of Swords swirls with inner turmoil. It is a moment of vulnerability, with the soul laid bare to its own demons. Guilt and fear lock muscles into immobility. Understand the source of those fears; learn what they mean and where they stem from. Know that the strength to break free of those shackles lies within one's own heart.

Ten

SHE FALLS. THE birds do not aid her. Instead, they circle in a tightening spiral around her. They wheel viciously above, like vultures awaiting the certainty of death. Their wings are like blades and their feathers are knives that slice skin and cloth alike. They pierce the shroud with their pointed beaks, facilitating the plummet to greater speed. Even their raucous cries seem hostile in the gray and indifferent night. The air rushes past her ears in a hollow and tuneless whistle. The trees below reach out bare-branched claws to the sky, their trunks rotting from within. *The end!* she cries out to the sky.

Or is it just the curtain falling upon an act of melodramatic martyrdom?

The Ten of Swords represents misfortune, desolation, burdens to bear, ruin, the end of delusions. It feels like circumstances have instigated a spiraling and uncontrolled plunge. Like her fall, sometimes circumstances are beyond human control. Sometimes there is nothing to do but ride it out and pick up the pieces when things finally come to a halt, and learn from the mishaps.

Page

$\mathcal{T}$HE PAGE OF Swords holds a cygnet in her embrace, her body a living cradle to protect it from harm. She has a strong sense of purpose. Mirroring her attitude, the swans gather close above to shelter her with their strongly beating wings as well. They are vigilant guardians. Their watchful eyes take everything in. Their wings beat in a flurry to create an updraft that carries her through the night.

She looks to the stars for guidance, following them as the sailors once did. The thin radiance of those distant points of light marks the trail to follow, as they have done since ancient times for those who know how to read their intricate patterns. Their webwork of light forms an arcane map. As she flies through the skies, they call to her and her companions and the winds themselves. In a rush, the winds come billowing to heed that call. She welcomes them; if those winds shift suddenly beneath her wings, she is quick to adapt. She is aware of those subtle changes and knows how to compensate for them. She beckons to you, inviting you to rid your eyes of the clouded haze of too much daylight, and to see the path that the nocturnal guardians of the sky offer.

The Page of Swords embodies honesty and truthfulness. She is unafraid to scrutinize her beliefs; she looks at the balance of black and white around her without condemning, and she knows the measure of her own soul. She is unafraid of emotion, though she does not let emotions rule the decisions she makes; logic is what dominates her the most. Her mind is agile and analytical, and she uses that to guide her sense of purpose and assess situations. She stretches her perceptions to try to make room for the new and unknown.

Knight

*T*HE KNIGHT OF Swords is the brave hero who rushes headlong into conflict to defend his beliefs. He is blunt and comes directly to his point. Dissembling is not something he is capable of. This can be seen as a refreshing honesty and true loyalty or a lack of tact and discretion.

He does not let emotion come between him and his purpose. Emotion in his matters is extraneous, muddying what is obvious, allowing room for doubt or fear. An emotionless knight is fearless, invincible, and does not acknowledge the possibility of defeat. He does not back down once he has engaged, for he knows no other option but victory.

This knight is a domineering personality. He rides upon the king of the birds, and together they are like a spear through the heavens. He is a seeker, slicing through the skies with his sword and his wings. A storm gathers in his wake, born of the turbulence his winged army creates, and he is lifted high above it all to pierce through the chaos. The sword is a beacon to his followers.

He calls out to the night's abyss:

> *Lift me up, spirits of sky.*
> *Grant me keen sight of Hawk,*
> *swiftness of Sparrow.*
> *Grant me insight of Raven,*
> *brave heartbeat of Hummingbird.*
> *Bear me up with grace on wings of Swan,*
> *guide me with visions of wisdom from Owl.*

Queen

*W*ITH HER BLADE, the Queen of Swords slices through lies and deceptions to the heart of truth. She is honesty and inner knowledge, sending forth her winged seekers into the world. They are an extension of her being and her soul. What they see, they send thrumming back to her along the invisible lines that connect them through the ether. They know the language of souls, for they have passed through a metamorphosis that is not sleep and is not death.

The blinding white is the color of purity, honesty, clarity, and uncompromising balance, but also of distance and sometimes death, for sometimes to get to truth one must cast off the old to slough off pretense and guile. Discard the past, leave the cocooning shells, and delve deep within to seek the true face to wear and show the world.

The Queen of Swords is an intelligent woman, loyal, witty, and humorous in her forthright way. She is valued for her accurate perceptions of the world around her and for her experiences. She has gazed within and knows that when she turns her eyes to a mirror, the reflection is exactly what it should be, and the light that shines within her soul blazes bright in the glass.

In the language of flowers, purple dragon lilies are symbols of inner strength, and white chrysanthemums, truth.

King

$\mathcal{L}$IKE THE VERTICAL sword he holds at the ready, he is a pillar of strength and morality. He holds power over life and death. He is a warrior king, sword always drawn so that he can be prepared to spring to action, should the need arise.

He is a leader, riding triumphantly at the forefront of his army. He carries through with his actions, following the path of truth that the blade lights for him. He is led on by the silent wisdom of the owl. She perches, balanced, upon the very tip of his blade, and her eyes swirl with all the ancient knowledge that her kind has been imbued with by human beliefs.

Mirroring the owl, he is also led by the shadowy ravens that trail at his side like Hugin and Mugin, Odin's twin ravens, "thought" and "memory." They fly away to seek out truths and bring their findings back to be whispered in his ear. In conjunction, they are the balance of night and day. They are the sharp clarity of the sun, and the owl is the truth that can only be heard distinctly in velvety light of stars and moon. This is what is embodied in those avian companions.

The shadows of the night descend upon his shoulders, a living mantle of purple, a color the ancient Greeks associated with royalty, and the base of the throne is etched with da Vinci's Vitruvian Man, symbolic of the blend of art and science, of the symmetry in the human body and in the whole of the universe.

Pentacles

Pentacles are the suit of the earth element.

Ace

*I*T IS THE possibility of prosperity, abundance, and security. It is the promise of wealth and well-being, of flourishing and reaping the rewards of hard work. Energy spent will see returns. A seed has been dropped into the fertile earth. What will sprout from that seed? What strange flora will burst forth? The suit of pentacles is a promise that something will come, but it will require patience and work. What grows is what you make of it. The seed must be watered and nurtured, for nothing grows in a void, and success requires more than dreams and fantasies. Water with desire, and nurture with faith and effort and diligence.

In ancient Egypt, the lizard was representative of good fortune and divine wisdom. They are the denizens of the earth and the guardians for the pentacles: salamanders, chameleons, dragons. They lead the way from nebulous dreams and the fantastic, ever-changing realms of desires and wishes into the reality of being, of tangible actuality, and of the world.

Two

HE STANDS UPON one leg and dances a juggling act of balance. Like the Hindu deity Shiva, he is engaged in the dance of creation and destruction, a harmonious equilibrium of opposing forces. As if his pose itself were not precarious enough, the rocky pinnacle he is perched upon seems ready to wobble and tumble into the abyss at the slightest incorrect motion or stray gust of wind; and yet he is confident. He knows this dance very well, can sense the dynamics of the situation, can feel the wind wending through with his movements like a silent and invisible partner as they perform an elaborate pas de deux. Will the confidence be his downfall? Will the zephyr lose its playfulness and traitorously strike before he can react to compensate for a swift change in the direction of its gust?

The Two of Pentacles is a balancing act: juggling and keeping everything in motion, being flexible and adaptable and changing directions easily. Meet these challenges that tumble your way with high spirits, but be wary of taking on too much at once.

Three

                  $\mathcal{T}$HEY WORK TOGETHER as one, creating a human ladder and climbing upon each other's shoulders. With their combined height, they reach upwards, they yearn towards the sky.

Into the stone wall, she inscribes her pentacles and her circles. They form a chain of overlapping arcs, like her interlinked relationships: circled sets of inclusion and combination. It is a mathematical equation of human relationships and interactions.

Each arc is inscribed with care, as if they follow a blueprint. Her fingers trail through the stone as easily as if the surface were malleable clay. The solid stone gives way under the soft flesh of her fingertips. Such is the power of their combined wills that what is "impossible" suddenly becomes easy, mundane, achievable. They comprehend the power of unity when one works in conjunction with others.

The Three of Pentacles is the embodiment of teamwork, of functioning together as a unit. It underscores competence and achieving beyond the expected. Sometimes the support of others is required to achieve a goal; not everything can be accomplished solo. Not everything *needs* to be accomplished alone. Reaching out to others is no failing, but working with others requires patience, planning, and compromise to adhere to standards of cooperation.

Four

$\mathcal{T}$HE DRAGON COILS tightly around his hard-earned hoard. He has spent many human lifetimes gathering up such a vast treasure. No one shall touch it; no one shall steal it from him! "Mine!" he hisses up to his tiny cousins who come creeping up to see. The salamanders and lizards scurry away quickly, lest he lash out at them in his possessive anger.

"My gold!" he declares. He knows the chameleons are watching with lustful eyes from above. He knows they are waiting for a moment of weakness to slip in and take. Even the light touch of wind feels like a thief stealthily attempting to creep up on him, and so he curls himself around himself, around and round and coiled tightly, tail to snout and endless coil. The salamanders scuttle off and leave him to himself. Burnished scales meld and become indistinguishable from the gold that he lies sprawled upon. Lovely, comfortable gleam, never tarnishing, never changing.

The Four of Pentacles embodies a possessive spirit, one who wants always to be in control. As a result, he lives within limitations, a cage of his own making, and is highly averse to any change. He is obstructive, in denial of his own weaknesses, chained by those very weaknesses. He is a miserly and miserable being who is financially well off but with a spirit that has been locked down by that preoccupation with his material state. Letting go of that selfishness might bring more happiness than that hoard has done thus far.

Five

SHE HUDDLES BELOW, curled in upon herself. Her eyes are downturned from the glory that spills out from the window made of liquid-colored light above her. Its beauty and color are reminders of her lack; she feels drab and drained by comparison. The dragon seems to trumpet exultantly, mocking her and demanding humility. Only the thorny ground embraces her. It stretches spiny tendrils towards her, and she shrinks way from it. She feels her solitude with an acute pain, not seeing the soul that hovers just at her fingertips nor any of the other eyes watching from the shadows.

She is oblivious to her surroundings, willfully blind to her external world, and ignorantly blind to her inner one as well. Her spirit cries with needs that she does not heed. Or perhaps it is that she simply does not understand what she really yearns for, so separated is she from her body and spirit's signals. There is disconnect.

The Five of Pentacles is indicative of spiritual poverty, material troubles, insecurity, and hard times. There is a neglecting of the body's needs, a feeling of being ostracized and excluded, of loss. And yet, salvation is not far off, if you can make that connection and see past the mental and physical blockades. Even the thorny bush that she views as her only companion bears flowers.

Six

HE SITS AT the pinnacle, upon the dragon's back, confident and self-assured. He knows that he has attained his heart's desire in this life and is brimming with riches. And so he plays a melody from that high-up perch. He lets his accumulated wealth pour forth in the song he pipes to rain upon the parched earth below. The dry soil cries for that relief, stretches thorny tendrils out to welcome the rain of life and the blessings in his song.

The Six of Pentacles represents the cycles of dependencies between those that have and those that have not. The sapling pushes through from the mud and muck and desolation under the shower of life and wealth from above. The piper does not see or notice it, thinks perhaps that he is part of a one-sided equation of generosity; but at the same time, the plants and branches buttress up the towering wall that he perches from. Their rootlets creep into the crevices and bind the structure with their mesh of life, protection from erosion, bracing. One supports the other, like an ouroboros, a self-sustaining cycle.

In such a linked circumstance, who is it truly that is the benefactor? Who holds the power?

Seven

$\mathcal{S}$HE STANDS IN the verdant garden that she has lovingly tended. She is the guardian dryad of the wood. She is a part of this place, this Eden of her own making. The peaches are ripe; a magical energy writhes in each lush globe. Peaches are a fruit of summer, of long days of relaxation. Their nectar is honeyed longevity. The sweet tang of their juice rolling over the tongue is like a visceral memory of summer.

To pluck them or no? The tattooed waves churn on her body with her speculation. She lays her hand on the fruit, ready to take it. It pulses faintly as if it contains the heart of the tree, beating with the pulse of sap through the branches. Will these peaches still sparkle with that living glow once taken from the tree, or will they just become dull as the normal fruit in her basket?

The Seven of Pentacles challenges you to make a choice: to eat and enjoy the fruit in the basket, or to leave them to flower and ripen and continue upon the branch? It is about reaping the reward for effort and work. The seeds have been sown; the time of work and waiting has passed. They have grown and come to fruition. Now is the moment to appreciate. It is a calm moment of consideration of alternatives and different approaches.

Eight

$\mathcal{W}$ITH DILIGENCE AND patience, the spider crafts her gossamer web. Dawn dusts an array of dewy stars across the threads.

Weaver, weave a pattern:
weave a dream of summer musk;
weave the drape of autumn dusk.

Weaver, weave a fate:
weave a life's frail, anchored line;
weave the pale moon's waxing signs.

Weaver, weave a web:
craft each silky, precious thread;
artist's inhibitions shed.

Spider works hard. She weaves her web through the night, each thread placed with care to create a pattern at once beautiful and built for a purpose. It is like a meditation, an intricate dance with eight legs: spin, step, step, hold, place thread, twist, and step; and repeat.

The Eight of Pentacles embodies a craftsman, someone possessing great patience and who is attentive to details. It is a call to be absorbed in a project, to seek out knowledge, and pursue a higher understanding. But this must be done with practical experience, using one's own hands and body and mind to create. This is often what is required to achieve success—a practical application of intellect and skill to a task to see through to the finish.

Nine

*H*ER SPIRITUAL BEING is in communion with the material aspects of her life. She strives to make that connection musically through such an elaborate and mechanical instrument as a piano—metal and wood and weighty mass somehow crafted to create order and beauty and ringing sound.

This piano, however, is no pure man-made one. It is tuned to the surrounding world. It is inextricably entwined into the fabric of nature, growing like the living trees around it do. It is a part of the forest, a part of the moss and leaves and bark, and the songs that trickle forth as her fingers fly across the keys echo with that influence.

She is alone. She comes out here to seek the solitude that the woods offer. She is content in her self-sufficiency. The snail shell she sits on and the spirals in the branches of the trees are a physical representation of the golden mean ratio, a continuum that approaches the infinite, approaches balance, approaches the ideal. She does not look at her hands as she plays but gazes up at the stained glass perfection of the sun shining through the leaves from above. She smiles and basks in the warmth and the emerald radiance.

The Nine of Pentacles is a balance of the material with the spiritual. It is material well-being and refinement, discipline in order to attain such, relying on oneself, and trusting in one's own abilities. It is understanding and appreciating the wealth that one already possesses.

Ten

SHE IS CLAD in silk and bedecked with golden adornments. Her rich attire indicates that she enjoys comfortable social status.

She curls herself up against the hoarding dragon as he uncoils and winds like a breeze above the valleys.

The winds whisper ancient secrets to the trees. The trees wrap their roots around their own nuggets and then, with a brush of leaves, pass it on to the dragon. And he in turn sings those words to her, for he has seen much in his centuries and has been steeped in what was. The world is a stained glass masterpiece—a world of art and wealth—and she holds clasped tight a peach, which has long been a symbol in China for immortality and auspiciousness.

She is a traditionalist, rooted to convention and to set standards, for she knows it is because she has played by those rules that she has been able to attain her position in life. She is aware that it is no random chance that has brought her here. There is a pattern to life and to the world. It is laid out like the stained glass that surrounds her—purposeful, crafted with a master's hand. This crafted vision is more enduring in its physical nature as a piece of art than as the more ephemeral realities it depicts. She knows that the heights she has reached result from her own hard work and beliefs.

The Ten of Pentacles is about enjoying affluence, desiring the permanence that financial security can bring and being able to appreciate luxury and the good fortune that has befallen you. This is the ultimate in worldly success, the result of long-term efforts finally brought to fruition, of finally being able to settle in to a lasting beneficial situation and position.

Page

OPPORTUNITY SLUMBERS LIKE the dragon upon whose crest the Page of Pentacles rests. Dreams and visions vibrate along its emerald length. They rise up through the soles of the feet of any who tread upon that viridian path, transmitted from the leviathan's sleeping mind—dreams of success and of being able to possess material comfort and stability. She knows those visions that the dragon offers—a wondrous garden of delights. She is the keeper of that garden, dedicated to its preservation.

The Page of Pentacles comes bearing her message for opportunities of growth and prosperity. It is a small spark she holds, but she is just the harbinger for potential. Make of that spark what you will—a mere smoldering coal or the blaze of a rising star—but that choice and vision is something that each individual must find on their own, using skills and resources at hand.

She is trustworthy, diligent, studious, and embraces scholarship. She is practical, down to earth, one who reflects before acting but at the same time is unafraid to embrace a world of physical enjoyment. She is lighthearted and joyous, and her spirit is entwined with everything around her.

Knight

*T*HE FOLIAGE PARTS for him in a narrow path, and he has eyes for none of the temptations that surround him. The spirits of the woods gather near and whisper temptations and dangle their faery baubles. The dryads stretch out their slender fingers to brush his helm as he passes beneath their outstretched branches.

But he does not notice; he has eyes only for the light that is his goal. The Knight of Pentacles is methodical, thorough, and unwavering. He rides upon the crest of an earth dragon, grounded and slow but undeniable in its progress; where he sets his sights will be reached.

He never charges in without first fully assessing a situation. He has the time and the patience to do so. He is conservative and prefers to do things in a tried and true way, not deviating into the unknown. It may appear that he lacks creativity or a desire to explore, but he places more value on the success of a venture than how that goal is achieved. He is dutiful, steadfast, and loyal, and holds true to his word when he gives it. When there is a task at hand, his patience and energy never wanes until it is complete.

The Knight of Pentacles is stubbornly set in his ways and on his path, locked onto his goal, with almost a tunnel-vision mentality. This may seem to be a failing, but it can also be incredibly effective. He sees and knows exactly what he wants and where his destination is, and he moves steadily towards it in an implacable way. When he reaches that goal, he strikes with all the force of the earth that is his to summon: the weighty might of giants, the thunderous roll of an earthquake, the thrusting of a mighty tree's roots through soil and stone.

Queen

*T*HE QUEEN OF Pentacles yearns to nurture and care for others. She is brimming with generosity and possesses a warmth of spirit that glows from her eyes. The fan of branches arrayed around her figure are reminiscent of the ten-armed Hindu goddess Durga, embodiment of feminine creative energy. She is dedication, a protector, and one who is reliable and trustworthy. She is secure in her material possessions and her position in life.

The Queen of Pentacles will lend her support to any who ask. She has strength that she draws from the very oak tree that she is a part of (or that is a part of her). She is willing to share the strength that is drawn down from the sustaining, golden power of life and warmth of the sun itself into her branches, and transmuted into purest energy.

"Carry this as a token and a reminder that I am always here," she says, taking a leaf from the boughs that whisper a singing susurrus from around her. They sigh in a hundred voices, an eerie harmony of the secrets that they hold for her.

King

$\mathcal{T}$HE KING OF Pentacles bears a seed in his hand. It gleams golden, with an inner light, and it pulses as if it contains a heartbeat that speaks with a humble promise to sprout. The leaves strain forth to bask in that radiance. The branches offer ripe, honeyed fruits, each luscious globe swelling with tantalizing, sweet juices. His branches strain upwards like the proud tines of a stag. He is at once man and tree and dragon; all intertwined, interlocked, entangled; he is a king of the material world.

This king is an enterprising individual, a man possessing of multifarious talents. He has the golden touch of Midas, gilding everything around him with a sumptuous gleam. When he lays his hands upon a venture, it is bound for success. When he sets his mind to an idea, it becomes polished brilliance. He is reliable and adept at what he does. He is a steady and solid support should you need someone to lean on. The eternal strength and stability of the trees is his to draw from. Roots spread far and deep, taking energy from the dark, loamy wells of the earth—from the caverns of the earth guardians, from the lairs of dragons, and from the ancient stones and bones of the deep. With that stabilizing force, he stretches branches and arms and aspirations to the stars.

He is an inspiration for success and still is generous and willing to share his wealth and fortune. Partake of the fruit he offers. He knows that wealth will be shared and shared again, and from those fruits, new seeds will sprout and grow to be mighty trees.

Spreads

One-Card Spread

Sometimes less is more. A remarkable amount of wisdom and information can come from just one card. And the beauty of this "spread" is that it can be used to answer almost any question. Simply ask your question and draw one card. For example:

What do I need to know today?

What should I get my mom for her birthday?

Should I go to that party tonight?

How should I approach my annual review at work?

Why am I feeling this way?

Three-Card Spread

This is a very flexible spread to get a bit more information or to see relationships between aspects of a situation. You can easily adapt the position meanings to suit your question. Try some of these or invent your own.

Past   Present   Future

Use this one to see what events or energies from the past are affecting the present, and what in the present might shape the future.

Situation   Problem   Solution

Use this one to gain insight into a troubling situation and a possible solution.

Decision   Choice 1   Choice 2

This one is to help when faced with a decision. It shows the heart of the decision and the most important things you need to consider about the two choices. This one is expandable; if you have more than two choices, just add more cards.

Situation   What to Do   What Not to Do

Use this one to figure out the best way to handle a tricky situation.

Celtic Cross Spread

The Celtic Cross spread is a very traditional and well-known spread. It provides lots of information about any situation. In this spread, it is interesting to compare the fifth, sixth, and tenth cards, as they all have to do with the future and outcomes.

```
              3                        10
   5          1          6             9
              2                        8
              4                        7
```

1. YOU: This card represents you.
2. CROSSING: This card (placed sideways) indicates the conflict.
3. FOUNDATION: This card illustrates the basis, or foundation, of the situation.
4. PAST: This card shows influences from the past that are affecting the present situation.
5. IMMEDIATE FUTURE: This card illustrates what is likely to happen next.
6. CROWN: This card represents the outcome you desire most in this situation.
7. YOURSELF: This is your self-image—how you see yourself in the present situation.
8. ENVIRONMENT: This card represents the influences of those around you; it can show how others see you in this situation.
9. HOPES AND FEARS: This card indicates either what you hope for or fear the most in this situation.
10. OUTCOME: This card indicates what is likely to happen if nothing changes.

Is Love in the Stars?

If you are looking for love and wonder if there is romance written in the stars for you, use this spread to find out.

1. READY: This card represents a way in which you are ready for love to come into your life.

2. OR NOT: This card shows a way that you are not ready for love. To draw love into your life, consider this card carefully.

3. DO IT: Turn to this card for advice on a step you can take to put yourself in the path of love.

4. STOP IT: Consider this card as a warning about something that you actively do to block love from your life.

5. OUTCOME: This is your answer. If it is positive and love is in the stars, paying attention to cards 2 and 4 will only make things better. If the answer is negative, work on the issues in cards 2 and 4 and strengthen the energy noted in cards 1 and 3. Then try this spread again and see if you haven't created a better outcome.

Will It Last?

If you are in a relationship and wonder if there is a "happily ever after" in store, this spread will give you a sneak peak. Be sure to compare the cards in the various positions to gain further understanding. For example, the top line focuses on the positive aspects of the relationship, while the bottom row illustrates the challenges, so that would be a natural comparison. The first and fourth cards show your hopes and your fears. Compare them. How are they different? How are they similar? The second and fifth cards are the hopes and fears of your beloved, and should be compared to each other as well.

```
    1    2    3
                   7
    4    5    6
```

1. YOUR HOPE: This card is what you hope will happen.

2. BELOVED'S HOPE: This card is what your beloved hopes will happen.

3. STRENGTH: This is the relationship's greatest strength.

4. YOUR FEAR: This card is what you fear about this relationship.

5. BELOVED'S FEAR: This card is what your beloved fears about the relationship.

6. WEAKNESS: This is something about the relationship that is weak.

7. OUTCOME: This card is the likely outcome. If negative, work on the fears and weaknesses, shore up the strengths, and see what happens. If positive, use this information to make a good thing even better.

Balancing Act

This spread was inspired by the Two of Pentacles card in *Shadowscapes Tarot*. It is a card about precarious balancing. In our lives, there are times when we must juggle many things: responsibilities, obligations, wants, needs, desires, etc. Sometimes these have to do with our external life, things that we do in our day-to-day existence. Sometimes they have to do with an inner balance of beliefs, thoughts, and feelings. This is a good spread for both of these situations. It helps you understand yourself and the environment that is surrounding and affecting your efforts. It also reminds you that even during these times of balance, nothing is ever truly stable. Everything is in the process of coming or going. As you maintain the illusion of balance, what really is being created? What actually is being destroyed?

1. YOU: This card shows you something that you need to know about yourself in this situation. It can be how you are positively or negatively affecting the situation or how it is affecting you.

2. CREATING: This card shows what is in the process of being created. This could be something tangible or intangible. It could be what you intended to create, or it could be something you weren't expecting.

3. DESTROYING: This card shows what is in the process of being destroyed. This could be something tangible or intangible. It could be what you intended to destroy, or it could be something you weren't intending on destroying.

4. WIND: This card, like the zephyr in the Two of
   Pentacles, represents the external environment
   that affects the situation. This card will show if it
   is beneficial or not. It will show if it is changing or
   remaining stable.

A Journey

This spread was inspired by the Eight of Cups and the Hermit
cards in *Shadowscapes Tarot*. Both of these cards focus on leaving
something, setting out on journeys, and seeking for what is miss-
ing. When you find yourself feeling hampered by your current life
or the world and you are yearning for something different but not
sure what, this spread can help you identify what is holding you
back and what you need to move forward.

Cards 4 and 5 may form an interesting message when read
together. Is there a connection between why you are taking the
journey and what is lighting your path? How do these cards relate
to the "destination"? Likewise, is there a connection between the
"leaving" cards and the challenge?

5
1   4 6 7
2   3

1–3. LEAVING: These three cards tell what you are leaving
   behind, what is no longer satisfying to you, or what is
   holding you back. There may be three distinct things, or
   the cards may work together to describe one thing.

4. WHY: This card tells you why you are being called to
   embark on this journey at this time.

5. STAR: Like the bit of star in the Hermit's lantern, this
   is what is guiding or leading you on your journey.

6. CHALLENGE: This card shows a challenge you will face on your journey.

7. DESTINATION: This card shows what you are moving toward. This is the place, for this leg of the journey anyhow, that you (or your higher self) wants to get to.

Message from the Universe

This reading can be a very powerful experience and is a great time to practice the "entering the card" visualization that you read at the beginning of this book.

4

3

2

1

1. BODY: This is a message from the universe to you regarding your body—the way you care for it, the way you think about it, the way you honor or don't honor it.

2. HEART: This is a message from the universe to you regarding your heart, the way you protect or share your love, the way you feel, or the role you let emotions play in your life.

3. MIND: This is a message from the universe to you regarding your mind, the way you use (or don't use) it, the way you see and think about the world, or the way you approach problems.

4. SPIRIT: This is a message from the universe to you about your spirit. Perhaps it is something you need to do for your spiritual well-being, a way to honor your spirit, or how you can let your spirit fill your daily life.

Dream Come True

If you have a dream or a goal that you'd like to achieve, this spread will be very helpful. It will show what you can use, what you need to watch out for, and what you can actually do to help make your dream come true. Pay attention to cards 4 and 5. See how they might make good use of the energy described in cards 1 or 2 or how they might overcome the aspect illustrated in card 3.

```
        6
     4   5
  1   2   3
```

1. STRONGEST ASPECT: This is the strongest aspect of your dream or goal and is something you can use to build on—a steppingstone to further progress.

2. HELPFUL ENERGY: This is very helpful energy that is available to you. It may not be strictly energy but could represent someone who can help (particularly if a court card turns up here), somewhere you can find information or resources, or some other source of help.

3. WEAKEST ASPECT: This is the weakest aspect of your plan. It is where you will need the most help, have the largest need, or have a challenge to face.

4–5. TO DO: These cards represent two things you can do—two steps you can take—to make progress toward your goal or toward manifesting your dream.

6. OUTCOME: This card represents the outcome if you take the advice of this reading. If the outcome is not what you expect or not what you desire, think more about your goal and the possible ramifications. Consider modifying your plan, and try the reading again.